Francis Jammes

on the life and work
of a modern master

• • • • • • • • • • • • • • • • • • •

Kathryn Nuernberger
&
Bruce Whiteman, Editors

The Unsung Masters Series at Pleiades Press
Warrensburg, Missouri, 2014
• • • • • • • •

ISBN: 978-0-9641454-5-0

Published by Pleiades Press
Department of English
University of Central Missouri
Warrensburg, MO 64093

Distributed by Small Press Distribution (SPD)

Book design by Wayne Miller. Series design by Kevin Prufer.

First Pleiades Press Printing, 2014

Our profound thanks to Wayne Miller and Phong Nguyen for their advice and support. Also to Brian Blair for his support and to our children, Alice Nuernberger Blair, Theo Whiteman Maynard and Severin Whiteman Maynard, who kept us entertained. —*KN & BW*

Invaluable financial support for this project has been provided by the Missouri Arts Council, a state agency. Our immense gratitude to this fine organization.

Contents

• • • • • • • • • • • • • • • • • •

Introduction

Bruce found Jammes by following his ear:

As a graduate student working on Pound's *Cantos* over thirty years ago, I remember noticing Jammes' name several times in various essays by Pound. I was already then a reader of French poetry, but my passions went more in the direction of Rimbaud, Lautréamont, and Baudelaire than in the fin-de-siècle, and I did not follow up on Jammes at that time. Perhaps I looked him up and, like so many readers, was dissuaded from reading his poems by the narrative of his re-conversion. It strikes me as absurdly superficial now to have shrugged off a fine poet merely because he became a devoted Catholic after his first books; but, well, I was a callow youth wild about Modernism and rather disdainful of the traditions of conventional religious poetry. (Blake was a different story.)

Much more recently, as part of my research towards a never completed dissertation on French art song and depth psychology in the period before Freud's advent, I discovered a series of letters in the Bibliothèque Jacques Doucet in Paris (Mss. 3666) written to Jammes by the wonderful French composer Henri Duparc (1848-1933), whose settings of Baudelaire and other poets I was already deeply passionate about. The Doucet will not allow photocopying nor will it permit one to use a digital camera to take photographs of manuscripts, so I had no choice but to sit in a reading-room at the Sorbonne (where the Doucet librarian arranged for readers to consult manuscripts) and transcribe by hand this interesting group of letters. Duparc's was a sad case. After studying with César Franck, and after a brilliant beginning when he wrote a handful of the finest songs in the French *mélodie* repertoire, he fell ill with what usually gets described as hyperaesthesia, an abnormal sensitivity to stimuli, and stopped composing in his late thirties. He lived for almost fifty years after his work largely ceased, and like Jammes, whose poetry he admired, he too re-converted to Catholicism. In any case, this series of letters inspired me go to the closest FNAC, where I found copies of Jammes' first two books, including the texts of the "Elégies" and "Tristesses," both of which I later decided to translate.

Jammes had not yet published anything during Duparc's active period of composing, so there are no Duparc-Jammes collaborations. But I soon enough learned that Jammes' poetry had been set by other composers, most notably Lili Boulanger, who set some of the poems from "Tristesses" as a song cycle called *Clairières dans le ciel*, published in 1919 after her death. Lili Boulanger also had a tragic history as a composer. She was the sister of the noted pedagogue Nadia Boulanger—the teacher of so many American composers among others—and was the first woman ever to win the Prix de Rome, France's highest musical award at the time, the one which Ravel infamously did not win. But she was ill much of her life, and died at the age of twenty-four of Crohn's Disease in 1918, leaving, among other projects, an unfinished opera based on a Maeterlinck text. She set only roughly half of the poems in Jammes' series (thirteen of the twenty-four), but her cycle is an extraordinary achievement. Darius Milhaud would later set the entire cycle of poems in the mid-1950s, when he was still teaching part of the year in California; but while his settings are good, Boulanger's far outshine his in passionate intensity.

It is often stupidly claimed that the worst poetry makes for the best song texts, on the argument that good poems have their own intrinsic music and are not easily set to a different one. But too many examples can be cited to support the counter-argument, not least among them Duparc's setting of Baudelaire's "L'Invitation au voyage," one of the finest French songs of all, not to mention settings by Ravel and Debussy of poems by Baudelaire, Mallarmé and other accomplished poets. The poems of Jammes set by Boulanger, Milhaud, and other French composers are admittedly somewhat simpler, at least in terms of content, than these examples, but their music is of a high quality, a quality that nevertheless did not stop the composers from reimagining them in a different musical context. To listen to "Elle était descendue au bas de la prairie," the first poem in "Tristesses" and the first in Lili Boulanger's cycle, is to re-hear a delicate music transformed. She does not vitiate Jammes' music; she gives it a different aural legitimacy and psychic compulsion.

Where music and poetry collocated are the concern, it is worth recalling Stravinsky's contention: "From the moment song assumes as its calling the expression of the meaning of discourse, it leaves the realm of music and has nothing more in common with it."[1] In other words, a great composer leaves a poem alone and tries to voice its quiddity in a parallel art form. The music does not interpret the meaning in any obvious way. Good poetry, then, is as open to a composer's music as lesser poetry (and that lesser poetry has been gloriously set to music is certainly true). Jammes was fortunate in his composers, as they too were fortunate in having his poetry to move them to composition. It has been a pleasure for me to discover and to live with both.

For Kathryn the road to Francis Jammes began with Marianne Moore:

After working my way through Marianne Moore's complete poems for the second time, I wanted something new to read that I would enjoy at least half as much and decided to start with her influences, one of whom, I learned, was the little known poet Francis Jammes. Translations were hard to come by, but there were a few rare offerings, first published in the 1960s and 1970s by Teo Savory, Barry Gifford and Bettina Dickie, that I was able to get my hands

1. Igor Stravinsky, *Poetics of Music in the Form of Six Lessons*, trans. Arthur Knodel and Ingolf Dahl, Preface by George Sefaris (Cambridge and London: Harvard University Press, 1977), 42-43.

on through interlibrary loan. And what a treat it was to discover Janine Canan's feature of translations and commentary in *Exquisite Corpse* and then to find that she had recently published a book of selected poems through a publisher in Australia.

Though quite different from Moore's poetry, I certainly enjoyed Jammes' work half as much and then some. While he was contemporary to the Symbolists, there was a crispness to his imagery, a frankness to his voice, and a strangeness in his sensibility that kept me reading. At first I thought of his mystical attention to a concrete reality and his facility in drawing correspondences between interior and exterior experience through evocative imagery as a proto-Surrealist impulse. However, essays in this book have convinced me Jammes' departure from the Symbolists is a departure that anticipated and then influenced the development of American Modernism.

In an arc reminiscent of W. B. Yeats' trajectory as a poet, Francis Jammes began his career writing excellent examples of nineteenth-century literary aesthetics, but instead of settling into the familiar voice and style that brought him so much attention and praise, he continued to experiment and to challenge his readers' aesthetic expectations. Unlike Yeats, Jammes' mounting mysticism and imagistic tendencies were dismissed by his French contemporaries as provincial dogmatism and the later work was disregarded. But, as a number of the essayists in this volume point out, American Modernists were still paying attention.

I speak some French and spent a great many hours reading French critical assessments of Jammes, but the conversation about his work petered out in the 1950s and Jammes increasingly became a slight footnote in the anthologies, at best. It was T. S. Eliot who first suggested that the literary canon is not written in stone, but is rewritten by each generation of writers, who claim some voices as influences and disregard others. In that spirit I sought out Bruce Whiteman, who had published a few very fine translations of the elegies I had encountered around the web and mentioned in his bio note in *Jacket2* that he was working on more. I contacted him to see if he would co-edit a volume on Jammes for the Unsung Masters series. It was a vision of a canon of the past constructed by writers of the present that guided us in seeking appreciations and commentary on Jammes from writers primarily known for their poetry, as well as academics and translators. These essays give some insight into what Jammes' place in literary history has been, but they also imagine what his place might become.

We hope you find as much to enjoy and admire in this collection as we have in our explorations of Jammes' life and work.

—Kathryn Nuernberger & Bruce Whiteman

A Folio of Writing by Francis Jammes

Jammisme: A Literary Manifesto

I

I think that Truth is the praise of God; that we must celebrate it in our poems for them to be pure; that there exists but one school, the one where, like children imitating a model of perfect handwriting as precisely as possible, poets conscientiously copy a pretty bird, a flower, or a girl with charming legs and graceful breasts.

II

In my opinion, that's enough. What on earth am I to think of a writer who delights in depicting a living turtle incrusted with precious stones?[1] I cannot believe that such a person is worthy of the name of poet, because God did not create turtles for this purpose, and because their habitats are ponds and the seashore.

III

All things are worthy of description when they are part of nature; but natural objects comprise not only bread, meat, water, salt, a lamp,

---

1. This is a reference to J. K. Huysmann's novel *À Rebours* (1884), in which the central character, Des Esseintes, sets gems on a tourtoise's back, killing it.

a key, trees and sheep, man and woman, and high spirits. Swans, lilies, coats of arms, crowns, and despondency, among others, are also included.

What am I to think of a man who, because he sings of life, wants to prevent me from celebrating death, or vice versa; or who, because he paints a thyrsus or clothes edged with ermine, wishes to prevent me from writing about a rake or a pair of socks?

IV

I find it perfectly natural that a poet, in bed with a solid and pretty young woman, at that moment prefers living to dying; all the same, if a poet who has lost every worldly possession, who has been struck down by a cruel disease, and who is a believer, composes deeply felt lines in which he asks the Creator to take his life away soon, him I think quite acceptable.

V

Many schools have come and gone over time (as the Buddha said, "I was led into schools, I know more about them than the doctors")—but to the founder of any given school, has it not always represented the vanity of watching a group of inferiors gather together to add to his personal glory? Could it be said that this is to advocate for some philosophical system in a selfless fashion? Such childishness, since one man's meat is another man's poison, and there is only the one system: Truth which praises God.

VI

A poet is therefore in the wrong to tell his fellow poets: You will always walk beneath linden trees; take care to avoid the scent of irises and not to taste beans: because they cannot love the scent of the linden, only the smell of the iris and the taste of the beans.

VII

But since all is vanity, and even this statement is another vanity, it is the right thing in this century for everyone to establish a literary school. I ask everyone wishing to join mine, in lieu of founding another, to send their subscriptions to Saint Peter Street. Orthez, Lower Pyrenees.

[trans. Bruce Whiteman]

These Are the Works

These are the works of man which are great:
To measure foaming milk into pewter pannikins
To gather ripe wheat-ears into sheaves
To cover fresh loaves with white linen napkins
In autumn to compost scudding leaves
To tap fiery maples for their syrup
To seek honey drunk by wild bees from the hyssop
To put new soles on old shoes in the winter-dark
room where the scarred cat and the blinded lark
doze in the chimney-nook near children at play
To answer the crickets' shrilling at dusk
with the loom's steady boom and creak
To herd the cows home at the close of day
To bake bread and tread wine
To husband the vine
To sit by stony brooks plaiting reeds …
In spring to turn soil for new seeds.

[trans. Teo Savory]

The Village at Noon

The village at noon. The lacewing fly drones
      between the bullock's horns.
      If you wish to, we will go
to the dun-colored fields now under plough.

Listen to the cockcrow... to the strike of the clock.
      In the paddock the donkeys bray
      the tree-swallow planes away
the water runs under a ribbon of poplars to the lock.

The well is choked with moss. Hear the chain
      as it creaks and creaks there
      when the girl with golden hair
pulls up the blackened bucket that drips silver rain.

The girl walks away leaning to one side
      the pitcher on her golden head
      her head like a gold beehive
mingling in sunshine with the flowers of that olive.

And see how the farmhouse roof of black slate
      shoots blue sparks at the blue sky
      and the lazy trees hardly sway
against the horizon under the noonday's weight.

[trans. Teo Savory]

The Useful Calendar

In the month of the Ram, sow thyme,
carrots, cabbages, peas, lucerne and clover.
Harrowing is over, and spading; it is time
to rake the beds and feed the trees, turn over
the earth under the vines, cut them back
and stake them, and to tie each stalk.

For the byre-animals, no more winter groats.
They can be led to the meadows now, the young
dark-eyed heifers, their coats smoothed by the tongue
of their mother, where they will soon find fresh oats.
The days draw out an hour longer, dusk is sweet;
at evening the trailing goatherd puffs his flute,
the goats pass by the working collie
who guards and keeps them from their folly.

[trans. Teo Savory]

A Child Reads the Almanac

Near her basket of eggs, the child reads the almanac.
Besides the Saints'-days and the weather to come
She can look at the beautiful signs of the Zodiac:
Bull, Goat, Fish, Crab, and *Ram…*

Country girls, in this way, can learn
That markets, too, are set up in heaven
Just like this one around her, with lambs,
Donkeys, cows, bulls, goats and rams.

Indeed, she's seeing the market of Heaven
And when she turns to the Sign of the Scales
She'll remember the spice-shop where there's leaven
For bread, coffee, and sometimes a conscience, for sale.

[trans. Teo Savory]

The House Would Be Full of Roses

The house would be full of roses and wasps.
In the afternoon, we would hear the bell ringing for vespers;
and grapes the color of translucent stones would appear
to be sleeping in the sun, below the crawling shade.
How I would love you there! I offer you all my heart
that is twenty-four years old, my mocking spirit,
my pride and my poetry of white roses;
and yet I do not know you—you do not exist.
I only know that if you were alive
and with me at the bottom of the meadow,
we would be kissing and laughing under the yellow bees,
by the cool stream, under the thick leaves.
We would hear nothing but the heat of the sun.
The hazel trees would shade your ear,
and then we would mingle our mouths, no longer laughing,
to tell of our love what can never be told;
and I would find, on the red of your lips,
the taste of the white grapes, the red roses and the wasps.

[trans. Janine Canan]

The Dining Room

There is an armoire, faintly shining,
that once heard the voice of my great-aunts,
heard the voice of my grandfather,
heard the voice of my father.
The armoire is faithful to these memories.
It would be wrong to imagine her always silent,
since I talk with her.

There is also a wooden cuckoo.
I do not know why he has no voice now,
and do not want to ask him.
Perhaps it simply broke—the voice
once in his spring—
like that of the dead.

There is, as well, an ancient buffet
that smells of beeswax and preserves
and meat and bread and ripe pears.
He's a faithful servant who knows
he must not take anything.

I have been visited by many men and women
who did not believe in these little souls.
I smile to think they envision me alone
whenever someone enters saying:
How are you, Monsieur Jammes?

[trans. Janine Canan]

First Elegy

For Albert Samain[1]

My dear Samain, it's to you I write again.
For the first time it's death's way I'm sending
these lines that some old servant of an eternal small town
will deliver to you tomorrow, in heaven.
Smile at me lest I cry. Tell me:
"I am not as ill as you think."
Open my door again, friend. Pass over the threshold
and, as you walk in, say "Why are you in mourning?"
Come again. You're in Orthez. Happiness is here.
Put your hat down on the chair there.
Are you thirsty? Here's some blue well-water and some wine.
My mother will come downstairs and say "Samain…"
and my dog will rest her snout on your hand.

I talk. You smile your serious smile.
Time doesn't exist. And you let me go on.
Evening arrives. We stroll in the yellow light
which makes the end of the day feel like autumn.
We skirt the swollen stream. A raucous dove
moans sweetly in a blue-green poplar.
I babble on. You go on smiling. Happiness is silent.
Here is the obscure direction we take at summer's end,
here we return on the simple pathway,
kneeling here near the *mirabilis* flowers in the
shadow that adorns the black doorways where smoke turns blue.

Your death changes nothing. The shadow that you loved,
where you lived and suffered and sang,
it's we who come out of it and you who stay inside.
Your light was born from this grim darkness
which forces us to our knees on beautiful summer evenings
when, sniffing out God as he passes by and gives life to the corn,
the guard dogs bark under the black convolvulus.

1. French Symbolist poet (1858-1900). He died of tuberculosis.

I do not regret your death. Others will fit the laurel wreath
there where it suits your wrinkled forehead.
Knowing you as I do, I would be afraid of wounding you.
There is no need to keep the glory of those who die
with unadorned brow from the sixteen-year-olds
who will follow your casket and weep over your lyre.

I do not regret your death. Your life is here.
Like the wind's voice that, rocking the lilies,
never dies, but returns years later in the
same lilies one had thought long faded,
your songs, my dear Samain, will return to cradle
the children whom our thoughts have already ripened.

For your grave, like some antique shepherd
whose flock is weeping on the hardscrabble hill,
I'd look in vain for anything to leave you.
The salt would be eaten by the gully sheep
and the wine drunk by those who stole from you.

I think about you. The day is fading like that day
I saw you in my old country parlor.
I think about you. I think about the mountains of our birthplace.
I think about that Versailles where you took me walking,
while we recited verses, sad and moving in step.
I think about your lover and I think about your mother.
I think about those rams which, on the edge of the blue lake,
waiting for death, bleated as their bells rang out.
I think about you. I think about the pure void of the heavens.
I think about endless water, the clarity of fire.
I think about the dew that glistens on the vines.
I think about you. I think about me. I think about God.

[trans. Bruce Whiteman]

Second Elegy

I

The flowers will glisten in the sun for me once again.
I feel like my soul is leaving a black country.
Can I find consolation under the trees?

My pipe is lit the way it used to be in my youth,
my pipe is lit in the noise of the rain,
and I muse upon spring days from long ago.

Cherished memories sweeter than lemon balm
fill my joyous heart, which remains sad,
like a garden full of young girls.

For it's to young girls that I like to compare
my thoughts, which are shapely like their timid legs
and have the ferocious mockery of their outbursts of laughter.

Young girls alone never gave me the slightest concern:
Who knows why, but their chatter is inescapable
there where the rain trembles in the wild rose.

As for me, my thoughts are inscrutable.
I should have been born on a calm day during the summer vacation,
when the raspberry bushes have white cousins.

I don't know why I've passed through life,
nor why, today, after pressing worries,
I am thinking again about evenings of love hidden by the rain.

My childhood is over there in a small flower bed,
my youth a grey-green autumn love affair,
nothing's left to come but the holly of the graveyard.

If God has spared me from death,
maybe it's because he remembered you, as a little girl,
waiting for me and taking care of your pretty canaries.

II

Ah, come, as the old poets used to say,
Ah! come… Let your little heart embrace me.
In the gloomy village, you'll see old lilac trees
with flowers as fresh as the movements of your head.
And if you haven't noticed the setting sun
disappearing in the blue mist that glimmers in the oak trees,
you will feel that sun burn on your mouth.

If you haven't seen the sweet dawn stitching up the night
and light up the angelica at the edges of the ponds,
I'll show you the dawn by closing your eyes
with a kiss as long as the dawn itself.
And your heart will be full of a white rising day
for I'll lay dawn itself upon your lips.

And if you haven't felt this pleasant sensation
that Zénaïde Fleuriot[1] called love,
I will explain it to you slowly, slowly,
as though you lifted your mouth to my mouth,
with your round knees pressed hard against mine.
Then you shall know this feeling which is called love,
a feeling rarely discussed that is constantly on everyone's mind.

Why am I so young, why in my unspoiled heart
is it like the frisson of evening in the hazel bushes?
I'm mad. I want you on the blue of the grassy earth,
around seven o'clock when the moon, high in the sky,
rains its first drops on the heads of the red cattle
whose horns still bear a tiny remnant of sunshine.

1. Nineteenth-century Catholic writer (1829-1890) of novels for young
women.

You'll know: You whom I knew as a very young girl,
am I refurbishing my dream out of next to nothing?…
I want to pummel you with clematis flowers,
I want to feel your throat surrounded by lilies,
and hear the cry of your outburst of laughter
rise towards a hail of my kisses.

Don't be afraid: From old poems we'll take
things once understood which then got confused,
words that now are but an obscure music.

And evening will melt into flickering daylight
in the depths of the kitchen where a servant who died
with a submissive smile on her face still seems seated.

The flowers have burst forth in full sunshine.
Dogs bark and the shutters overlooking the wisteria
open onto a thatch of sleeping leaves.
Your lithe, gliding arm will cease to be numb,
and our tired eyes will see a swirling cloud of love
on the plain beneath the icy blue water.

Isn't it true that you will fear for my sudden suffering?
Don't ask me. I can't tell you.
You mustn't ever know why I spoke of so many others.
I've loved no one but you since hearing the thrushes
rush in from the North to peck at reddening autumn.
Its winds are as bitter as olives.

Do not pry, and if you know how to love me,
let your sweet silence fill my bitter heart.
If we go for a walk, listen thoughtfully then
as though you were hearing it for the first time—
the endless, dry and broken noise of leaves
that turn as they fall on the forest floor.

Think of me no longer, think of me no more.
There was a sweet name "that recalled autumn."
Oh my dear, I love you. But don't ask...
See this translucent crocus and that pink mushroom.
Your light feet will move over the moss of dawn
where the pure grains of the dewy hour gleam.

"Tell me, dear... Say nothing, for I love you.
I don't want to know what I know. Be silent.
It comes back again, the time when you were younger,
when the roof of your house used to sing
under the May rains. Love me. Love me."

"But tell me only whether the woman whose name
reminds you of autumn is still alive?"
"Don't make me speak, sweetheart."
"But do you love her no longer?" "Remember the statue of the Virgin
which stood in a niche on a neighborhood corner?
Her belt was blue and her hands were broken."

Back in that lovely time, on Sunday evenings
the whole town broke out in little fanfares.
High school prefects escorted younger kids.
The sweet smell of incense wafted in the squares.
You took your younger brother home.
You gave him your pale, fine-veined hand,
and off and on the slits of your black eyes blinked.

Ah!...I am thinking about you again. Are you yourself or someone else?
The caresses planted in my heart have flowered.
Today feels like that lovely time long ago.
My pain gives birth to blue hollyhocks.
If you want them, you need only put out your hand.
Water them a little. They'll revive tomorrow.

III

And I thought about you again this morning.
I looked at the poor little purple deadnettles.
It's autumn, yet it seems like the month of May.
The ivy smiles at me. And in this age-old garden,
I'm still that young man, tender and a bit old-fashioned,
who at first light, in his room, would read
the old botanical book with passionate drawings.

If you accept my soul for what it is,
some green evening come fetch it beneath the linden trees.
The day has returned when, in the little town,
one rainy summer night, sad and alone, I'd watch
the procession go by that was supposed to ward off
the floods that threatened in the fields.

Yes, darling, I go back to my lovely childhood.
My soul is as pure as a soul can be,
like the gleam of silver on your cheeks,
like the trembling azure light
on the white pathway around eleven o'clock
that sets the thick black rose and the weeping iris afire.

My sleep is purer than any night of romance.
Sweet lover, I want your heart to cleave to mine during those light nights,
in the six-day Spring when night calls to itself,
when the day is endless and the lost song of the
nightingale fills with a disconsolate joy
the lilacs which want to die but cannot.

But my fantasy is this, that before you find me
you will go quietly from room to room
talking to the old things that will narrate my life.
But say nothing to the specimen box
where the flowers of my adolescence lie sleeping.
Those flowers still preserve the reflection of forests

from days of overwhelmingly mournful summers.
Ask nothing of it, for its lasting perfume
could die of joy in the realization of who you are.

Sit down for a moment at my little table.
I've set out some books there on an old shawl.
My inkwell glimmers there as the day fades away.
A yellowing almanac is far out of date.
These are bitter days, faded days,
as sweet as the journal of Eugénie de Guérin.[2]

In the corner you will see the camphor-wood trunk
on which as a child my grandmother used to lay me to sleep,
and which now rests undisturbed after a tempestuous
sea voyage more than two centuries ago,
with the thoughtful uncle who returned from the Indies,
with only the memory of a woman in his heart.

You can pose questions to its mysterious wood.
It will tell you stories of a dreamy little boy.
They are pure and will not offend you, my dear.
It was in sleeping on this old fragrant chest
that my heart filled up with tender young girls
and oriental trees where snakes took refuge.

May your hand in passing brush against my
grandfather's solemn letters for their blessing.
He sleeps now beneath the blue air of Guadeloupe
amidst the cries of the ocean and the shore birds.
Tell him you are off to find his grandson.
Your frail grace will make his soul smile.

You will understand the charm that obsesses me,
of what old flowers my soul is comprised,
and why in my voice old-fashioned romances

2. French writer (1809-1848) whose journals were published in 1861. Her
brother, Maurice de Guérin (1810-1839) was a well-known poet.

seem, like a dying sun, to hang on,
like those ancient and gloomy young people
whose memory lies in the October of rooms.

Then you'll come to me. You will press your heart
to mine, lithe and graceful, and without a word
you will recognize my deep joy if I weep,
and all you will have to do is to smile gravely
and press your weightless soft body against mine.

For you I'll be as sweet as a young girl.
My heart will have that deepest blue of leafy bowers
where some older sister gave her brothers snacks,
and from which, at the end of the afternoon, you can hear
the shiny scythes being sharpened on the whetstone,
in the midst of the eternal silence of the prairie.

IV

Rain falls from the sky in a deluge on the wet leafy spearwort.
Right at this moment, I feel sure, you are sewing near the fire.
The shadow of the room where you sit trembles, and subtle
     gleams of light
ricochet on the faded black mahogany of the furniture.

The day we were born it was already a given that
I would compose these lines amidst the noise of this rainstorm,
and that against the green tiles I would see once again
your grave profile, full of love and sadness.

It was preordained, oh sadness, oh beloved.
And what does God know today about our future?
Who can say? The water falls drop by drop in the grey air.
The fire crackles. I am calm and you are there.

My soul rejoices at having nothing to say,
at composing these lines with scarcely a thought.

They are just like your old grey dress,
they are just like Ash Wednesday.

...But I've already spoken about your house.
I cannot say enough about it when October
comes back, and it is my sweet and monotonous folly
to be like your flower when this season returns.
In a few days once again I shall be in the village
where you are, and in the scent of cold evenings,
I want to restore my passionate, sad soul to you,
when the storefronts glimmer on the sidewalks.

I'll be the schoolboy I used to be,
I'll light the same wooden island pipe
I used to smoke in the fog of the grey neighborhoods,
when school started again amidst the renewed smell of books.

But won't you find that I've grown too old?
At twenty-seven I miss being seventeen.
I've never felt this with such keenness...
Yet my dream is young and so is my smile.

I've given away so much of my youth—too much, really—
but enough remains for me still to suffer.
It seems gone to me, and I feel it renewed
like a denuded thicket where a May wind blows.

And besides that, what else do I do today?
That wind was the one that blew under my door.
I've come to find you again, because I need you.
...But I must pay attention to what you say...

Don't move from the old armchair at the edge of the fire,
the one that's too big for you and where I'm sure you make
the needle gleam on the stiff and twisted tapestry.
Is the mateless bird still in the large cage?

I will say nothing to you. Please just let me
astonish myself for having forgotten you.
It's as though I've had a high fever for the longest time.
I need your sweet, tender seriousness.
Don't reject me. Hide within yourself
whatever is there. Don't tell me you love me.
Go on pushing the needle, grave and single-minded.
Then lift your eyes in my direction for a moment, and say nothing.

Composed at La Roque, in September 1898.

[trans. Bruce Whiteman]

Third Elegy

This countryside has the soft freshness of a stream's edge.
The paths are lost in deep obscurity, moss-black,
leading into blue depths full of remembrances of love.
The sky is barely visible at the tops of trees too tall.
It is here, among friends, that I come to walk
with my sadness, and that beneath the sun I
crawl slowly alongside the flowers and grow less bitter.
They are disturbed by my heart and its sorrow,
and I am at a loss in responding to them.

Perhaps when I am no more, a sweet child
will remember having seen a young man pass by
on the pathway, wearing a sun hat and
gently smoking his pipe on a summer morning.

And you whom I left, you will not have seen me,
you will not have seen me here, thinking about you
and dragging my glum heart as big as the woods…
And besides, you won't understand, no, you won't,
for I am far from you and you are far from me.
It is so easy to forget your pink and white mouth.
So why do I go on suffering?

Dearest, if you have the answer, come and tell me.
Tell me why, when I am in the depths of despair,
why does it seem like the trees are as ill as I am?
Will their death come with mine?
Will the sky die? Will you?

[trans. Bruce Whiteman]

Fourth Elegy

When you asked me to compose an elegy
for this abandoned country where the high wind
makes the sad white birch trees rustle in the grey sky,
once again, in the green shade of the wet thickets,
I saw a rumpled dress with long ribbons.

From the green grass of the park, under the cold dead sun of October,
a broken Diana rose up like a fountain.
The false pistachio trees, the red hazel nuts,
the lacquer-trees, the laurels and the roses
produce a sad and beautiful passageway at the horizon
where blue emanations stain the sky.

Death gently revived in my soul again.
I thought about all those who passed their lives there,
the children who feigned slaughtering the lilacs,
the barking clang of the bell for mealtimes,
and the crows cawing in the soft grey sky
where the weathercock pointed west, a sign of rain.

The young girl had her room on the south-east side, near
the lane of yew trees, not far from the green-water fish pond.
The furniture in this room was made of maple.
A thimble and a pair of scissors gleamed on a table,
and in the blue window glass where leaves could be seen
a mended pier-glass reflected little blue cupids.

Gunshots could be heard out on the open fields,
and the dining-room had folding screens.
The porcelain tiles bore yellow birds.
Cold noontime meals in the waning days of September
were passed in an endless and depressing silence,
and when the young girl came down from her room
she would kiss her fussy old grandfather's brow.

Doubtless it's her dress that my dreaming invokes
on the bench eaten away by the moss and the moist air.
It is still at the end of the darkest path,
among the pine needles, pliable and dead.
It is there that Celia, leaning sadly on her elbows,
would come after lunch to sit in the pale sun.

You wanted to see the house again in my company.
Better than I you knew the dreary story
of this Celia who died of languor,
succumbing to an illness whose name was kept hidden,
a sickness about which rumors were rife,
rumors which the servants carefully put to rest.

And we went under the long dead leafy cover,
up to the window which we opened
by pulling the iron wire from the rotten wood.
Then we found ourselves in the blackened kitchen,
so black it seemed that soot burned
in the icy hall from a square of night.

The steps had holes in them from dampness.
Frozen powdery rust was flaking
from the ancient keys hung beside the locks.
From there we heard the high wind in the road,
that depressing wind marking the end of the vacation,
groaning its story among the sycamore trees
that, as they die, take on the color of the dawn.

You said to me: "This is Celia's room."
Of the furniture only a broken mirror remained,
still mounted in the woodwork. You said to me: "The wall hangings
    illustrate some amazing subjects."
You could see Roman chariots beloved by Bonaparte's somber Empire,
the vicious period when in fake repentance
the Nucingens traded love for political gain.

You pushed a shutter back against the wisteria.
There on the wall slept the bell with the dead sound
that used to be rung just before meals.
You pulled lightly on that bell's clapper
and its mournful voice, slow so it could be heard,
wept in the soul of the room as though in mourning.

May Celia's soul rest in peace.
In the park where she used to go I will pick some roses,
red arbutus and ground lilacs.
Reverently I shall lay them at the foot of the mound
where she was buried one October day.
May Celia's soul rest in peace.

[trans. Bruce Whiteman]

Sixth Elegy

It was such a humble landscape for your beauty.
From the church, boiling hot yet cool beneath the ivy,
a bell kept up its slow beat, like a failing heart.
A lamb bleating at God, sweet-tempered and grave,
had the soul of a prayer in its whiteness.
A mangy cat, cowering in an old passageway,
a poor hunchbacked child, a sparrow in its cage—
you pass near them with your proud high spirits
and your dress fetchingly tucked up.

And me, I bow before you, climbing the
shabby street at the foot of the mountain,
prostrate and wanting to die before these signs of wretchedness.
You've never understood this instinct I have
to relinquish your loveliness for a moment…
But I can see the bird madly battering its cage,
that cat and this hunchbacked child, one after the other,
full of God's spirit in spite of everything.

And you placed your delicate hand on my shoulder.
And slowly I raised my eyes towards your lips,
then turned them away to look again at
a black doorway where a demented old woman stood trembling.
And the bell went on sounding over Sunday's gloom.
The softness of your flesh mixed in my soul
with the misery of poverty, in a white prayer
sweeter than the clear voices of children holding branches.

You did not understand the words of my silence.
And hearing them again, you said: Dearest, are you a little sad?…
Can I console you? Shall I read to you…
I said nothing, and from my room you took
my beloved copy of *Paul and Virginia*[1]

---

1. Bernardin de St. Pierre's late 18th-century *Rousseauiste* novel.

which on the blue hillside where I felt so loved
I had filled with flowers like a school girl.
And my heart grew calm, conjuring up the sweet child
with a large hat of shaddock flowers,
his feet turning silver in the moss,
with my dog Fidele, and Domingo, and Marie,
with night fallen on the hut that prays,
and the wings of the flowers in the hummingbird plants.

Your slow voice, a bit affected, would endure in
my soul, like a mortal kiss.
You closed the book and saw me crying
as though it were Rousseau's day when everyone cried all the time,
that sad time, when they sang of sublime feelings
made courageous (remember Countess d'Hourdetot![2])
by hymns to the eternal unhappiness of lovers
who, reunited too late, alas, departed too soon.

…Then your face glowed like the white bell-shaped petal
of some flower evoked in dream by the soul of the pond.
You pressed me against you, silent and solemn.

A dizzying swell of deep blue, brought down the mountain stream,
burst out on the mute rocks on which the clear water kept its eye.
Out the open window we could see the stiff farmers
passing by on their way to mass.

Their gestures were slow and stiff, and their voices
sounded like a short loud echo, while their steps
were regular on the hard ground. The sound
beat on the air. And the old ladies in colored shawls
bright as toys went by with their kids ahead of them.
And the distant snowy peaks seemed to collapse
in the glacier of a heaven of transparent stone.

---

2. The Countess d'Houdetot (1730-1813) was a French woman with
whom Jean-Jacques Rousseau fell in love in 1757.

My heart, oh beloved, burst forth then.
The poverty, the suffering, this reading,
the grave mountain people striking the hard ground,
all of it reminded me of the places of my birth.
In my heart I felt the winds of Bigorre,
the white ascent of the flock towards dawn,
the tall red shepherds' crooks in the shade,
the scattered brush fires in the mist,
and the restless dogs, the donkeys and the flutes,
and night noises, and God's calm.

Oh give me your love! Put your hand on my breast
and breathe all the love in my heart.
Stony hillsides are part of me, and ravines,
whole villages full of dark sorrows,
flocks bleating at the white blueness of the hilltops.

And part of me too, oh my sweet darling,
is your smile which quietly brightens
the mean street where my soul has fallen asleep.

November 1898

[trans. Bruce Whiteman]

Thirteenth Elegy

When the organ is played just for us
        in the church,
there will be drops of deepest blue beneath her eyelashes,
        tears of the fortunate woman.

But where is the woman pure enough
        for my soul, which is like a country
church bell buried in the aristolochia flowers?
        Where are you, my Intended?

If only the soul of my white June roses
        breathed on your lips of Bengal rose:
wash your body, o trembling one, don your sandals
        and come.

Quit the bitter world and enter the little room
        of my self-communion,
where running water can be heard in the mint
        consumed by the white sun.

Awaiting you is the greeny freshness of my dreams
        where sheep lie sleeping.
Awaiting you is a necklace of white beach stones
        washed clean in well water.

If you are tired when you arrive, I will kneel down
        and unlace your sandals.
Just lean your head on my shoulder,
        and I will carry you along.

The white room filled with a golden din
        will celebrate your advent.
On my bed where I stretch you out,
        rest and dream of water's freshness.

And weeping with love, I'll go off into the white solstice,
      my worn-out dogs in tow,
to ring the flowery bells of the simplest churches
      to mark my Intended's arrival.

[trans. Bruce Whiteman]

Fourteenth Elegy

Darling, you said. And I replied, Darling.
It's snowing, you said. It's snowing, I said.

Again, you said. And I replied, again.
Like that, you said. And I said, like that.

Later you said: I love you. And I, I love you more.
Lovely summer is over, you said to me. It's fall,

I said. And our words had got out of synch.
At last one day you said: Oh dearest, how I love you...

(It was a day when the long fall was fast losing its grip.)
And I said back to you: Say it again...and again...

[trans. Bruce Whiteman]

Fifteenth Elegy

To Henri Ghéon[1]

In this book of flowers I found a dried herb
put there one Sunday fifteen years ago in Bordeaux
on an evening as pale and scented as a peach.

Bordeaux is a beautiful place where boats
sound their horns amidst showers of soot.
It was there that Mme. Desbordes-Valmore[2] took ship.

She must have got on board among orphaned girls,
standing at the bow of the boat with disheveled hair.
She must have sung "Le Rivage de Maure" in a low voice,
wracked with sobs and making a theatrical gesture.
How she will have touched the captain's heart,
he who was used only to fevers, typhoons,
huge waves and cannon volleys.
He will have kept an eye on her, the young poet,
who grew pale when she felt the ship heave.

Did she take a cat with her in her humble cabin,
or a canary that she had raised herself
and for which a little fresh water was kept perhaps
during the sadness of the long crossing?
In the poor orphan's wallet
would a few pennies remain after passing the Equator
to pay its baptism among the sailors, dressed for the occasion?

Heart of mine, do not smile at this poet.
She was the genius doomed to suffer endlessly,

---

1. French writer and friend of Jammes, 1875-1944. He was also a close
friend of Gide's and helped to found the journal *Nouvelle Revue Française*.

2. Marceline Desbourdes-Valmore (1786-1859), a French poet and actor.
She was a close friend of Balzac and was the only woman whose poetry
was included by Verlaine in *Les Poètes maudits* (1884).

whose anxious tears and their bitter salt
make her red eyelids smart and plastered her hair.
She was the exile who gave herself to the winds,
understood only by the rainbow-hued hummingbirds,
whose arms with the harps of the Empire
grew old in vain beneath long regrets.
When she left the ship in the blessed Antilles,
with the black flame in her hollow cheeks,
she surely sought out some modest hotel
where she could eat what people eat
who sigh dejectedly when they have to pay.

And I, I bow to her memory, she
whom a dried herb has brought back to mind today.
But when I am dead and gone, who will
remember me as I remember Desbordes-Valmore?

[trans. Bruce Whiteman]

Seventeenth Elegy

For Madame Eugène Rouart[1]

It has rained. The fresh earth is content. Everything shines.
A drop of water hangs heavily from every rose,
but it will be hot, and this afternoon,
the buzzing sun will crack the reddish earth.
The foggy sky is full of blue holes like water
from which sun rays fall at an angle on the hillside.
The glossy-skinned mole with strong claws has filled in
his underground burrows that riddle the lawn.
The silvery snail has crossed the road,
the soaking-wet fern is heavily bent over,
and the brambles have rained down on the necks of young girls...

For they've set off, those young girls, towards
what is wet, and trembling, and green.
One had her crochet work, the other a lively mouth,
yet another an old book and a fourth some cherries.
Another had forgotten to say her prayers.
"Lucy, look at all those molehills."
"Oh how ugly that snail is. Step on it."
"Oh God no. I don't want to."
"Listen, is that the cuckoo singing?"

                                    They passed on
to the top of the road where it leads to the heath.
Their dresses wafted airily up and then down.
The silences of their clear voices mingled together.
A magpie slowly crossed the sky. A blue jay
chattered as he followed another jay into a black oak tree.
Like a fan the dresses wafted up again
in a wave, in the full sun at the top of the road.

---

1. The wife of Jammes' friend Eugène Rouart (1872-1936), a writer and
editor. She was painted by Renoir and photographed by Degas.

They're gone now. It makes me sad to think about it.
Feeling old, for no reason at all
I picked a bit of mint from the ditch.

[trans. Bruce Whiteman]

Selections from the *Tristesses*

I

In this shadowy light that falls at midday
on the sleeping vine, when the hen
has laid her egg in the dust, I desire her.
Above the clothesline where laundry is drying,
I'll see her face rise up, open and clear.
She'll say: I feel poppies in my eyes.
Her room will be ready for sleep,
and she will go there like a bee to its
cell made white by the heat.

II

She went to the bottom of the meadow,
and because it was all in flower
with plants whose stems thrive in water,
I picked them, those water-sodden plants.
Soon, wet through, she climbed to the top
of that meadow all in flower.
She laughed and shook herself with the
awkward grace of a young girl unused to her body.
The look she gave was like lavender.

IV

She is quiet and happy. Once in a while she will
look up as though to catch me thinking.
Sweet in that moment, she was like the yellow and blue
velvet of a row of pansies late in the day.

V

I'm sad at times. Suddenly I think of her.
Then I'm so happy. But I grow sad again
not knowing how deeply she loves me.
She is the young woman with the transparent soul,
who in her heart jealously nurtures
the profoundest passion given to one alone.
She left before the lime-trees bourgeoned,
and when they blossomed after her going,
I was stunned, my friends, to see
lime-tree branches with no flowers.

VII

Memory of her fills the air so clear it felt like
the shadow of a bird passed over my head.
The tulip-tree in the park was a raw green-black.
A nameless beauty fills the blue air from the tops
of misty pine-trees in the far distance.
In the front room where she used to visit,
where we kept cut lilies dark as night,
now there are roses in a glass
and a sprig of magnolia placed by my
mother on the sunken polished piano.
The flower has not opened yet,
but it is swollen and ready to burst,
rising above the vase as though
bidding fair to fly off amid summer.
I close the window to keep the shadows in.
I'm thinking. I've suffered. I'm lost. I'm thinking.
The pump creaks and my dog sleeps on the floor.
Will the day come when, unlatching
the front door that dreams under the cedar,
her hand will make all the light of her presence
flash across the worn tiles of the room?

VIII

At the foot of my bed, my mother
placed a statue of the Black Virgin. I like
this Virgin and her somewhat Italian religion.
Our Lady of Loreto, erect on a base of gold,
who makes me think of the thousands of fish
sold on the docks where barely a breath of air
blows over the stalls that are so sleepy.
Our Lady of Loreto, know that in these hours
when I feel unworthy of her love,
your perfume revives my poor heart.

X

If this is all just a pitiful dream, and if in my life
yet again I must pile
disillusion on disillusion;
and if again, in my dark delusion, I must
seek out in the softness of the wind and the rain
the sole empty voices that hold my heart fast:
dear love of mine, I may never get better....

XI

I have no interest in the fiery passions.
No: she will be as sweet to me as autumn.
Her purity is such that I desire
her to wear daffodils on her hat.
Only, if she must grant me the favor
that pure virtue makes calm and blessed,
and watch over what I do like an ant,
I see her smile at me from the garden
among the red peppers deep in September's color.
They'll force me to recall old passions.
She'll be the lily who ruled over all of them.

XIII

Our love shall be greater if we say nothing
when we meet again, extending our hands.
The limbs of ancient trees will cast their shadows over you
on the bench where I know we will sit together.
It's there that your friend, that village sprite,
with all the grace of her eighteenth-century forebears,
kind as one is when one has truly suffered,
it's there in the heart of that green sheltered place,
that she spoke of you to him who loves you.
So we shall sit on this bench, just the two of us,
when the sun, casting purple shadows on the squirrel,
sets on the lawn amid the brood mares.
Love, for the longest time you will not venture…
How sweet you will be to me, and how I will tremble…

XIV

Was the weather fine when your lover died?
Oh! How I wish I knew whether it was morning...
Before taking her leave, did she smile at you?
Give her the edelweiss you no longer want...

XX

Two columbine flowers stood swaying on the hill.
And one said to its double:
I tremble in your presence and remain confused.
And the other replied: if I look at myself in the
rock that the water is wearing away drop by drop,
I see that I too tremble and am confused.
Increasingly the wind rocked both flowers,
filled them with love and melted their blue hearts together.

XXIII

Come, my beloved, come, my little lamb,
for the blue water will sleep in the meadowsweet...

XXIV

Tomorrow a year will have passed since I picked
the flowers I spoke of in the wet meadow at Audaux.
Today is the most beautiful day of Eastertide.
I took refuge in the blue of the countryside,
through the woods and meadows and fields.
How have you have survived a whole year, my heart?
Yet again, my heart, I have put you through the misery
of seeing the village where I suffered so much,
those roses shedding blood before the rectory,
the lilacs that slay me in their gloomy beds.
When I recall my ancient distress of the heart
it's a miracle that I don't cast myself
face-first into the yellow dust of the footpath.
Nothing left. I have nothing, nothing to sustain me.
Why is the day so lovely, and why was I born?
If only I could rest on your quiet lap
the weariness that wrests my soul that lies
in restless sleep like a beggar woman in the gutter.
To sleep. To achieve sleep. To sleep forever
beneath blue rain showers, under new thunder.
To stop feeling. To forget about your existence.
To lose sight of the hillsides engulfed in blue
in that crazy azure mix of air and water,
and of the void where I seek your presence in vain.
A profound absence at the core of my being
seems to break out in a great mute sob.
I write. And the land is full of a joyful noise.
The bells calling us to Vespers can be heard,

and the crickets chirp amid the happy peaceful countryside.
In the wan rooms of rented farms
work-clothes hang silently near the flour sieves.

She went to the bottom of the meadow,
and because it was all in flower...

[trans. Bruce Whiteman]

From *The Four Books of Quatrains*

Purity

As countless swarm the wisteria, despite
frost on the walls, hunting nectar, lost,
a stray cluster confusing the air, the pale sun,
your blond hair. Everywhere white.

Solitude

On the mountain where Boudachourry
and I go. He's thin as the wind
and young with seventy years' poaching.
Does it matter if he gets my heart wrong?

Cunning

Bourdachourry, hunting in worn sandals,
a black pipe in his teeth, shakes his fist
at game that will not show its face.
The moment the hare bolts, he cuts it down.

The Long Stretch

Bourdachourry said to me: I used to leave
at dawn, hunt all day, then hunt all night,
then the following day and the night once more,
until I came before the forest at Iraty.

Vertigo

The emptiness around me forms mountainous heights,
the sheep scatter, all this makes me tremble.
My dream: a little hamlet tucked away
over the church at sea level, a balustrade of tranquility.

Nocturne

The southern wind blows a path around
the garden, under the sleeping moon.
He pulls back the long lace curtain.
Every life lives on just this side of nothing.

Downpour

The slick road shines as I pause to dry
my beard. And my waterlogged boots groan.
Watching the passing rain, sheet by sheet,
the house erased from the top of the hill.

Saint Mud

I know now, Heart,
your secret.
A clod of earth
mixed with tears.

Bird Flight

A curve of thread across the morning,
 a woodpecker is a kind of shuttle
stitching tree to tree,
hemming the garland of blue.

The Four Seasons

So it rains a silvery fretwork along the irises,
so it rains far and thick, a mist quenching the dust,
so it rains like veils over a psalm—*De profundis*—
so it rains on snow that melts before touching down.

To My Goddaughter Sylvette Guillon-Verne

You returned from the depths
of the earth, the sky, then the dew
evaporated off lilies, not even damp,
not even, close as it was, smudged with dirt.

Farm Wives in the City

From the rain and the mud they descend,
from hills of gorse and broom sheared by bovine
teeth, jamming their troublesome strong fingers
in white gloves, they have all the allure of a plow.

Their Royal Highnesses, The Infantes

With a song of grief echoing from out of his court
the southern wind comes whipping around the violet coats,
shadows pleat them, a little mountain range
flowing from the Pays Basque into Spain.

Minotaur

They spent all yesterday working on the thresher
and couldn't get it to hum.
But look at her now, how she swells and bellows
devouring sheaves of hair, plaited and luminous.

Far from the Salons

It was a brutal day in the chaparral
when we saw the wild horses passing
and that dog tied up, reluctantly picking
at a dead lamb the shepherds abandoned.

The Banquet

The ceremonies at this table feel almost holy,
what with a blood-red table cloth adorned in lilies,
the flag beaten by the winds,
an old Basque song drowning out the clinking dishes.

[trans. Kathryn Nuernberger]

Images

The abbey in Tournay, the village in the Pyrenees where Jammes
was born.

"Portrait of Francis Jammes" (ca. 1898) from *The Book of Masks* by Félix Vallotton, a Swiss painter and printmaker (1865-1925).

Francis Jammes.

(Notice au verso.)

A young Francis Jammes, taken around 1910.

Francis Jammes with André Gide. A friendship and lifelong correspondence between these two writers began in 1893 and lasted until Jammes' death in 1938.

Ginette Goedorp on the day of her marriage, October 8, 1907, to Francis Jammes. Together they would raise seven children.

The home in Orthez that Francis and Ginette shared
from 1907-1921.

Jammes on the banks of the River Pau in Orthez around 1920.

Portrait of Francis Jammes by Dornac on June 7, 1919.

Jammes with his dog, Sultan, in Hasparren in 1925.

Francis with his mother around 1930.

The poet in his study around 1930.

Essays

Francis Jammes: Poet of the Pyrenees

(from the introduction to *Under the Azure: Poems of Francis Jammes*)

Janine Canan

One hundred years ago in the French Pyrenees, a poet wrote lyrics of extraordinary pure feeling. His name was Francis Jammes. His joyful, however sorrowful, poems express an innocence and simplicity as natural as the song of a bird or the love of a child. "The essence of Jammism is tenderness, purity, mysticism, and a love of nature that saturates all this sweetness of feeling with the smell of the earth," Robert Mallet wrote in his biography. "With you," Paul Claudel wrote to Jammes, "everything is original and virginal."

"To be true, my heart spoke like a child," Jammes said.

Against the current of sophisticated, rarefied Symbolism prevalent at the end of the nineteenth century, Jammes' seemingly simple, incantatory poetry of the heart, with its childlike expression of desire and lament, delight and praise, struck contemporary novelist André Gide as pure audacity. Yet even the greatest of the French Symbolists, Stéphane Mallarmé, had to admire the country poet for his "delicate, tactful, naïve and unerring verse with its exquisite network of voices."

"I have loved Francis Jammes because he does not separate art from life," wrote the young writer Alain-Fournier, whose own life and art were sacrificed in World War I after the publication of his first novel, *Le Grand Meaulnes* (*The Lost Estate*). Years after Jammes' death, novelist Jacques Borel called him *the poet of existence*: "an existence at once ordinary and enchanted…woven with dreams that contrast with a fresh and searing sensuality."

"You don't read Francis Jammes," Gide commented, "you breathe him, you inhale him. He enters through your senses like those Spanish balsams whose leaves and stems are as fragrant as their flowers….In Jammes' work there is nothing but poetry and perfume….Once you abandon yourself to him, you think he's the only poet there is."

Francis Jammes was born on December 2, 1868, in Tournay, a village nestled in the hundred-fifty-million-year-old Pyrenees mountain range whose eleven-thousand-foot peaks originally bordering a tropical land of dinosaurs, today separate France from Spain. According to the Greeks of the first millennium BCE, the Pyrenees were named after the fire goddess Pyrene, daughter of King Bebryx. Not far from Tournay is Lourdes Grotto where fourteen-year-old Bernadette Soubirous had visions of a Lady in white, only ten years before the poet's birth.

Francis' parents, Anna Bellot, the daughter of Alpine merchants and nobility, and Louis-Victor Jammes, the son of a French physician in Guadeloupe, moved to Saint Palias in the Basque country. Louis-Victor had been appointed town registrar, when their son was eight years old. That same year, Francis received, while at school, his "initiation in poetry":

> A book lies open before me. Suddenly without warning, I see and realize that the lines are living…And so I received from Heaven this reed, shrill and dull, humble and sublime, sad and joyful, sharper than the dart of a savage, sweeter than honey.

At ten, Francis Jammes entered the *lycée* in Pau where he resided with his maternal grandparents. Two years later his family moved to the port city of Bordeaux, where he spent his adolescence immersed in botany, Jules Verne and Baudelaire. The young poet fell in love, failed the baccalaureate, and composed eighty-nine poems entitled *Moi* (*Me*).

The day after Francis' twentieth birthday, his fifty-seven-year-old father, who had been ill, passed away. Anna took her two children back to the mountains to Orthez, the birthplace of their paternal grandfather, the doctor who had emigrated to Guadeloupe in the Caribbean and died before Francis' birth. Anna's older child, Marguerite, soon married, while Francis found temporary, if unappealing work as a lawyer's clerk and continued to live with his mother, as he would for the rest of his life. In the evenings, mother and son read Homer, Virgil, Cervantes, La Fontaine, Rousseau and Hugo. In 1891, twenty-three-year-old Francis published fifty copies of *Six Sonnets* (*Six Sonnets*), produced by a local printer.

A few years later, with the support of several established writers—Mallarmé, Gide, Loti—Jammes' *Vers* (*Verses*), a slim volume of free verse, and *Un Jour* (*One Day*), a play in verse describing a day in the life of the poet, were published in Paris. By then, Francis had already composed some of his loveliest and most unforgettable lyrics, poems steeped in a lush feminine imagery Claudel called "delicious and poignant." The haunting, delicately transparent "Mill in the Cold Woods" that ends "and I will pass through the woods / where that white girl holds her dress above the water"—describes what will eventually emerge as a typical jammesian moment of luminosity fusing woman, nature and the past. The vividly sensuous portrait "She Attends the School"—"that beautiful girl so white. / She comes in a small carriage under the branches, / during vacation when the flowers bloom"—is even more characteristic. From this early period also comes the exquisite, well-known lyric "I Love in Times Past":

> Come, come, my dear Clara d'Ellébeuse.
> Let us love again, if you exist.
> The old garden has old tulips.
> Come naked, oh Clara d'Ellébeuse.

Jammes' first work appeared in the 1890s at the height of the *Belle Époque*. In 1894, the same year that *Verses* was published, a small feminine face, finely sculpted from a twenty-five-thousand-year-old ivory mammoth tusk, had been unearthed near a cave at Brassempouy in the Pyrenean foothills. It was, and still is, the oldest representation of a human face in the world. On the south side of the Pyrenees in Spanish Catalonia, Picasso was painting his portraits in pink and blue, on the north side in French Catalonia, Maillol was starting to sculpt strong bronze women; while near the Mediterranean, arthritic old Renoir was absorbed in his voluptuous French bathers; and to the north, Monet was designing the sumptuous Giverny gardens he would be painting for decades.

Impressionism was in full radiance. Proust was ruminating *Remembrance of Things Past*, Bergson was concocting *Creative Evolution*, and Mallarmé composing his final masterpiece, "A Roll of the Dice Will Never Abolish Chance." In Ireland, the last of the Romantics, W. B. Yeats, born just three years before Jammes, was singing his sublime dreams to Maude Gonne. And from across the Atlantic, the lanky, free, open, optimistic verse of Walt Whitman was striking a deep chord on the Continent. As the nineteenth century rolled into the twentieth, a brief golden era produced phenomenal creativity and innovation: the invention of the automobile, the telephone, the phonograph, the motion picture, the airplane and the subway; the birth of Einsteinian physics, Kochian medical microbiology, Freudian psychology, and Picassoan art—even the Norwegian Nobel Prize. The French Empire had attained its greatest expansion.

In 1895, twenty-six-year-old Francis Jammes experienced an epiphany:

> It was during the month of April, 1895, that I was invaded—I can find no other word to express my meaning. A simultaneous explosion of all my lyrical powers took place within me. I do not know why I did not die from the blast of that violent wing which seemed to strike me, and from which my poem "Un Jour" was born.

The young man journeyed to Paris, where he met a group of

artists that included the painter Eugène Carrière; the next year he traveled to Algeria to join the novelist André Gide. Around that time, Jammes fell in love with a young Jewish woman whom he addressed as Mamore in his "Seventh Elegy." "Tell me, tell me," he pleads, "will I be cured of what is in my heart?" And she replies, "Beloved, the snow cannot be cured of its whiteness." In "It Was at the End," Mamore becomes Amaryllia who walks at his side, bitterly observing "the little rich girls." After two years, purportedly for his mother's sake, Francis ended their relationship.

In 1897, Jammes published his *Manifeste de Jammisme* that proclaims the hedgerows his school, the fields and flowers his academy. "Truth," he states, "is praise of God." His first major collection, *De l'Angélus de l'aube à l'angélus du soir* (*From the Morning to the Evening Angelus*) was published by Mercure de France in 1898. A generous gathering of freely rhymed lyrics on love and nature, full of compassion for the poor and reverence for natural beauty, *Angélus* embodies the force of youthful desire, and the power of imagination to overcome separation , loss and loneliness. The book opens with an epigraph, eventually set to music by Arthur Honegger, announcing the poet's call to his "métier sacré":

> Among men, I was called by You, my God, and here I am who suffer and love. I speak with the voice You gave me and write with the words You taught my parents who taught me. Like a donkey I walk down the road with my head lowered, laden with bundles, making the children laugh, ready to go when and where You wish.

From the Morning to the Evening Angelus brought the poet both controversy and wide acclaim.

In the following years, Jammes travelled to Provence, the Alps, Holland, and Belgium where he joined "Poets Against Literature." In Paris he met the religious poet Paul Claudel—younger brother of the sculptor Camille Claudel—who would become instrumental in his return to Catholicism. In 1901, Jammes published *Le Deuil de primevères* (*Mourning Primroses*), a collection of elegies and prayers balanced on the transparent line dividing poetry and prose, composed in the throes of depression over his failures to secure a lasting love relationship. His darkly ironic "Prayer to Love Sorrow" conveys the depth of his suffering:

> Oh my Sorrow, you are better than a beloved.
> For I know, on the day of my death
> you will be there, lying in my sheets, oh Sorrow,
> still trying to invade my heart.

In this state, Jammes experienced a religious illumination and in 1905—the year that France, amid considerable anti-clerical sentiment, passed the Law of Separation of Church and State—the poet "returned" to the Catholic Church. Until then, he had seen himself as a life-affirming pagan:

> I was christened a Catholic, but that was as far as my Catholicism went, that and my sympathies for its beautiful literary themes…I was a pagan, a veritable faun. Flowers, woods, women—I was in love with all that lived!…Before I experienced Grace, there were trials, and there was Claudel…

His next work, *Clarières dan le ciel* (*Clearings in the Sky*), published in 1906, revealed a marked shift toward a more religious vision, as Jammes attempted to integrate his new Catholicism with his old love of Nature. *Clearings in the Sky* culminates in a 38-part "Church Cloaked in Leaves" which in turn climaxes in the profoundly beautiful and moving "Rosary." This unique, quasi-pagan, quasi-Catholic chant was a marvel to Gide, Claudel, and other contemporaries. Half a century later, the popular song-writer Georges Brassens would create, from five of its stanzas, his much-loved "Prayer." Jammes' poem includes fifteen devotions to Mary, and since the traditional French rosary, interestingly, does not follow the abbreviated Latin *Ave Maria*, or English "Hail Mary," but rather the complete first person sentence structure common in the chants of Sanskrit (e.g., *Om Parashaktyai namah*, "I bow to the Supreme Shakti"), the ancient root-langauge of French, the recurring *Je vous salue Marie* can be literally translated "I salute you, Mary."

In 1907, Jammes published his *Souvenirs d'enfance* (*Memories of Childhood*), seventeen charming, sometimes ironic sketches of a country childhood now reviewed from an expanding spiritual perspective. "Mon cœur, mon cœur," he writes in one poem, "mon cœur, mon cœur, ô mon cœur!" in another of these outpourings of the heart. These *Souvenirs* are Francis Jammes' "songs of innocence." They reflect, as do other poems of his, the tender religious iconography that developed in France during the two millennia following Jesus' crucifixion in Jerusalem, despite the harsher aspects of a Christian Church that has also sanctioned crusades, wars and the burning of women. As in other French art, the archetypal images of a powerful Father, compassionate Mother, innocent Child and suffering Savior, are here steeped in the much, much older Nature and Goddess lore of neolithic and Paleolithic Old Europe. To this ancient, indigenous, matriarchal apprehension of life Jammes, however Christian, remains faithful.

Later that year, at the advancing age of thirty-eight, Francis Jammes married a twenty-four-year-old literary admirer by the name of Genviève ("Ginette") Goedorp. Engaged at Lourdes, the couple was wed in Geneviève's hometown Bucy-le-Long, and settled in the town of Orthez. Madame Jammes soon gave birth to a daughter who was christened Bernadette. Six more children followed: Emmanuèle, Marie, Paul, Michel, Anne and Françoise (who would become Sister Marie-Maïtna).

In 1912, Jammes published his prize-winning *Géorgiques chrétiennes* (*Christian Pastorals*). His play *La Brebis égarée* (*The Lost Lamb*) was set to music by Darius Milhaud, who during his lifetime would compose dozens of vocal works based on Jammes' poetry. In Paris, the poet was introduced to Anna de Noailles who literary salon was attended by such luminaries as Paul Claudel, Jean Cocteau, Colette, Léon Daudet (son of Alphonse) André Gide, Max Jacob, Pierre Loti, Frédéric Mistral and Paul Valéry. When Proust's *Swann's Way* appeared in 1913, Jammes sent his praises to the author he considered "the equal of Shakespeare and Balzac." The admiration was mutual. Proust was enchanted by Jammes' impressionistic imagery—"a sincerity and clarity of vision that could disentangle and evaluate the exact sensation, the precise nuance, affecting him"—and saw the poet as one of the greats.

In 1914, Germany declared war against France, and Jammes, now in his mid-forties, was appointed the ambulance administrator for Orthez. Deeply saddened by the loss of many friends, he nevertheless continued to write, publishing *Cinq Prières pour le Temps de la Guerre (Five Prayers in a Time of War)*, and *Le Rosaire au Soleil (Rosary in the Sun)*. A part of his cycle *Tristesses (Sorrows)* was now set to music by the composer Lili Boulanger, under the titles *Clarières dans le ciel*. In 1917, Jammes received the French Academy's *Grand Prix de littérature*. And in 1918, he finally met Marcel Proust—at a reception in the home of Madame Alphonse Daudet where Milhaud's musical renditions of Claudel and Jammes were performed. A few years later, Proust, from his deathbed, would ask Jammes to pray for him, for "a death sweeter than my life has been." In 1919, Jammes' *The Virgin and the Sonnets (La Vierge et les sonnets)* appeared.

In spite of the *Grand Prix de literature*, Francis Jammes never became a member of the Académie Française: his candidature was refused in 1920 and again in 1924. In 1921, the poet moved to a house in Hasparren, in the lower Basque Pyrenees, bequeathed to him by an unknown woman at the suggestion of a priest. There he wrote his three-volume *Mémoirs (Memoires)*—which was followed by a fourth volume years later after his death. That same year, Gide wrote in his *Journal*:

> There are certain poets, of whom Jammes is perhaps the only one among us today, who, it seems, would have written their work just the same in whatever period they had been born....I hope for the honor of France that he could only have been born a Frenchman—but all the same I can see him writing his *Elégies* at Tibur under Augustus, his *Jean de Noarrieu* anywhere wherever; he has a very definite local flavor, it is true, but in China he would have had a Chinese flavor....His spirit is the spirit of Jammes, not of Orthez....

In 1926, Jammes was awarded but turned down the *Légion d'Honneur*, saying that although he appreciated this attempt to compensate for the Academy's refusal, "a poet's work needs no official sanction, and the love the poet brings it, and receives in exchange, surpasses all other rewards." That same year, Jammes published *Ma France poétique* (*My Poetic France*). In "The Poet's Prayer," Jammes asks to be filled "like a tall glass painted with insects and flowers /...with the water of candor that flows to the foothills from the peak." Over the decades, many pilgrims—Francois Mauriac, Darius Milhaud, Alain-Fournier, Anna de Noailles, Saint-John Perse, as well as many lesser known admirers—had voyaged to the Pyrenees to taste that pure mountain water. In 1928 the master poet and philosopher Paul Valéry came to pay his homage as well.

Jammes was sixty-six years old when his mother passed away in 1934. In the following year, he wrote *De Tout Temps à Jamais* (*From Always to Forever*) and *Sources* (*Springs*), ten decasyllabic, ten-line poems in honor of ten sacred springs. These were the last poems to be published during his lifetime. *Springs* ends with:

> One beautiful noon, when my soul flies away
> to God and the angelus sets loose its petals,
> clear and blue as a lilac: may a vapor
> rise like delicate incense from you,
> oh my spring of Ursuya; may it follow
> the breeze that blows to the house
> of my birth and let its fresh voice fall
> in rain on my roof. May it accompany,
> for an earthly moment, toward heaven
> my song celebrating you.

Springs was followed by *Cinq Idylles* (*Five Idylls*) and *Feux* (*Fires*), final paeans to Life grounded in the elements of the earth, poems that would not be published until after his death.

By now a figure of fond reverence for the younger generation, James was awarded the Academy's *Prix d'Aumale* in 1936, and spoke at the Théâtre des Champs Elysées the following year. He had followed the path of "eternal poetry," he said; he had sought to affirm "simple Being"; he had not sacrificed feeling to form, which ought to be so transparent that it dissolves in the light.

On November 1, 1938, death pounced as Jammes had predicted, "like a young hawk on a hare blanched by many winters." The sixty-nine-year-old poet, sick with colon cancer, said to Jean Labbé, the young friend who brought him water from the Ursuya spring: "I no longer need to pray, my suffering is a prayer. I offer it entirely to God, the rest belongs to humanity." Francis Jammes passed away on All Saints Day at his home Eyhartzia in the Pyrenees, leaving over a hundred books containing nearly eight hundred poems, twelve novellas, four volumes of memoirs and several verse plays; a correspondence with many notable French authors of his day, as well as a significant influence on contemporary writers abroad.

JANINE CANAN is the author of eighteen books of poetry, translations, essays and stories. This essay is an excerpt from her introduction to *Under the Azure* (Littlefox, 2010), a volume of her selected translations of Francis Jammes available from Little Fox Publishing. She is also the translator of *Star in My Forehead: Poems by Else Lasker-Schüler* (Holy Cow! Press, 1999). She lives in California, where she is a practicing psychiatrist.

Sweetness

Christopher Howell

Francis Jammes was born the commencement of the Franco-Prussian war and died in 1938, one year shy of the onset of World War II. In the center, between the two, was the great tragedy of World War I and the resultant annihilation of what had remained (plenty) of genteel nineteenth-century European culture.

An aspect of that culture that did not quite disappear was the Symbolist movement in literature, a mutated form of Romanticism that pried poetry away from ornamented discourse and description and proposed the primacy of the inner life over the life of social forms and predictable formulae of value. It brought the magical into the mix, claiming it as one of the imagination's inalienable rights.

In France it represented also a turning away from Parnassian rectitude, and a return to the lyric tradition which, again, valued most highly the subjective experience over objective considerations, presentation over proposition. Charles Baudelaire (1821-1867), with his spiritual anarchism, his disgust with every tame idea and formulation, was symbolism's patron pioneer. In his *Intimate Journals* he wrote:

In certain semi-supernatural conditions of the spirit, the whole depths of life are revealed within the scene—no matter how commonplace—which one has before one's eyes. This becomes its symbol.

So anything might be made, or discovered, to possess symbolic force, depending on the readiness of the poet's spirit to encounter the shock of it—and the truth of it, Mallarmé would have said. Such readiness required an openness to ambiguity and immediacy of both language and experience. This might, of course, lead, as in Verlaine's case, to wildly extravagant conduct, or to textual opacity—a charge from which few of the Symbolists were exempt. Or, it might lead, as in Mallarmé, to intricate abstractions, unusual musical and phonetic constructs, a disregard for traditional understandings of the word, the line, and the page, and whole galaxies of symbolic confluence and value.

Though it seems contradictory, in Mallarmé's work, as in that of Claudel, Verlaine, Valéry, and the other Symbolists, masters of ambiguity, there is also the peculiarly French obsession with purity (what would, in Surrealist terms, become The Absolute). It is more obvious in the writing of the Parnassians than in the Romantics, and clearer yet in the Symbolist and Surrealist work. In Symbolist terms purity applied principally to the image; ideally, it was neither pictorial nor narrowly referential, but was itself a powerfully resonant event independent of equivalencies. Its purity resided in its force, undiluted, singular as a hammer. The trick for the Symbolist poet was to compress as much of this lyric force as possible into every line; which practice is chiefly responsible for the continuing impression that Symbolist writing is "difficult." It does not satisfactorily decode. Then there is Mallarmé's injunction (as paraphrased by Louis Simpson in *Modern Poets of France*) that the language of poetry must be different from that of speech—which is like a coin passed from hand to hand.

Poetry must never state a thing explicitly, it must always suggest: 'Suggestion makes the dream!' Poetry should be like music, and yes, poetry should be written in symbols…like constellations, the meaning flowering into the spaces between.

Though he was a sometime visitor at Mallarmé's salons at the apartment on the rue de Rome in Paris, Francis Jammes was in many ways an atypical Symbolist. Where most Symbolist work was nervously urbane, he was unabashedly pastoral. Where theirs was compressed, frequently his work was loosely composed; and certainly he often employed what Mallarmé would have thought of as the language of speech. In much of it he seems to have chosen "purity" over ambiguity. Where most of the Symbolists, Claudel excepted, were determinedly agnostic, Jammes was, from 1905 on, a devout Catholic. In fact, in spite of the judgments of Pound, Mallarmé, Gide, and Proust, Jammes was, in much of his work, scarcely Symbolist at all and thought of himself as a "Naturist." In his *Manifesto de Jammisme* he declared that the hedgerows were his school, the fields and flowers his academy.

It is no surprise, then, that I should have been somewhat confused upon first reading Jammes' work. I had heard him mentioned in connection with the Surrealists. But I know a bit about the surrealist group under the iron fist of André Breton and could not imagine that the gentle and retiring Jammes had ever been that close to them. I had found him more frequently referred to in connection with the Symbolist movement. But, initially, I had some trouble with the poems. The long sequence of elegies in particular was periodically laced with mid-nineteenth century romantic fluff: "cherished memories," "shepherds," "beautiful summer evenings," "sweet dawns," "pleasant sensations," "swirling clouds of love," "lovely times," "wafting fragrances," and many another chestnut. Again and again we come upon "sadness," "beauty," "heart," "suffer," "love," "joyous," "embraced," "no longer," "for the first time," "for the last time," "when I was young." I frowned a good deal through the initial reading. Yet, after several more readings, I was surprised to find I had developed a deep affection for Jammes' poems. How do the poems pull this off? In two ways.

In the "First Elegy" he addresses his dead friend Albert Samain in terms that seemed openly sentimental:

My dear Samain, it's to you I write again.
For the first time it's death's way I'm sending
these lines that some old servant of an eternal small town
will deliver to you tomorrow, in heaven.
Smile at me lest I cry. Tell me:
"I'm not as ill as you think."

But in rereading the poem I was struck by the speaker's candid invitation to Samain to return from death to visit as he had always done, to take with him the same walks on the same summer paths they had always walked as friends. What seemed at first textbook denial, the first stage of grieving, turned quickly to acknowledgment:

I do not regret your death. Others will fit the laurel wreath
there where it suits your wrinkled forehead.

The very rapidity of this movement, the sureness of it, helped me see the poem not as a mere epistolary conceit, but as an actual heartfelt address, and a declaration of faith in the power of human affection. This meant that where the language seemed conventional, it had seemed so because I had been relating it to the context of conventional literary usage, whereas Jammes actually means what he's saying, that it is not sentimental but, in a sense, innocent, luminous with an almost child-like candor:

Open my door again, friend. Pass over the threshold
and, as you walk in, say "Why are you in mourning?"
Come again. You're in Orthez. Happiness is here.
Put your hat down on the chair there.
Are you thirsty? Here's some blue well-water and some wine.
My mother will come downstairs and say "Samain…"
and my dog will rest her snout on your hand.

He goes on imagining Samain's visit, even after admitting his death and claiming, eventually, a triumph over death by virtue of friendship's deathless affection:

I think about you. I think about the pure void of the heavens.
I think about the endless water, the clarity of fire.
I think about the dew that glistens on the vines.
I think about you. I think about me. I think about God.

And here is the kind of language a reader might expect from a Symbolist writer, language forming that hermetic connection between eternity and existence, between the earth and the heavens, the human and the divine, in each case the human sensorium being the agent of connection. In this immense context, "Why are you mourning?" becomes a seriously resonant question. What is more resonant, ultimately, is the speaker's yearning coupled with affection, that it brings out of the experience of the poem a form of purity, a prime Symbolist value. It is a characteristic result of Jammes' poems and it is what, more than anything else, makes him a Symbolist, though he takes a not quite Symbolist path to it. Even in the poems that are frankly erotic there is this child-like quality, this alchemy of yearning, affection, and acute perception:

Her purity is such that I desire
her to wear daffodils on her hat.

Purity is Jammes' faith in the singularity of persons, objects, animals, scenes, memories, friendships, poems. It is a point of view Post-Structuralist criticism would come to disparage as "essentialist." Certainly such a view may have its dark side: Germany's National Socialism was built on it. Its moral and ethical expressions tend toward the black-and-white fundamentalism that is both fragile and dangerous—look no further than radical Islam or extreme Christian fundamentalism.

But this is not what happens to it in Jammes. In his work the instrument by which purity is apprehended is neither reason, as in Rousseau, or holy or unholy writ, as in Cotton Mather; it is feeling, and the feeling he seeks is not self-importance or gratification, but a sense of the wondrous. I realize "feeling" is a rather indistinct and unpopular word in serious discourse. And it may be argued that all poets make use of it. Yet it is not quite so. For many of the

Symbolists, and many modern and contemporary poets, it has been more a by-product than an instrument, Mallarmé being a good example. It is dangerous to use it as an instrument, as did James Wright, for instance: one's work may be dismissed as sentimental, soft, even passé.

Whether this feeling, or feeling tone, as expression, is sentimental or totally fresh is irrelevant to the speaker of the poems. The result, certainly in the elegies, is that there is a kind of continuing balance between candid declaration and Symbolist invention, and this balance is the second element in Jammes that brought me around to admiring his work. At the end of the "Seventeenth Elegy," for instance, the speaker observes school girls on a country outing:

> For they've set off, those young girls, towards
> what is wet, and trembling, and green

The erotic charge in those lines aside, at the end of the poem, there is an interlacing of pastoral nature with erotic nature, so that they become one thing, a single condition and result:

> A magpie slowly crossed the sky. A blue jay
> chattered as he followed another jay into a black oak tree.
> Like a fan the dresses wafted up again
> in a wave, in the full sun at the top of the road.

The eye is drawn one way by the slow drift of magpies, another way by the chattering jays, the dresses acknowledging, almost conducting, the scene, all of it blessed by the sun. It is a flowing and fresh language, balanced quickly by what in another writer would be the impossibly sentimental, "They're gone now. It makes me sad to think about it." Which he immediately rescues with:

> Feeling old, for no reason at all
> I picked a bit of mint from the ditch.

"These are my feelings," the poet says, "and here's how I came to them. And now I give them to you, with a taste of mint. See how my declarations, my ruminations, if you like, are verified by the imagery comprising the road that leads me to them."

So the sentimental, "It makes me sad…" becomes the naïve, is purified by its own vulnerability and candor. The result, in poem after poem, is sweetness, not a result conventionally associated with Symbolism or, indeed, with Modernism in general. We just don't believe it, after the butchery of two world wars, the genocides, the revelations of psychology and neuroscience regarding human perception, motive, and pathologies of normalcy. Yet Jammes, who lived until 1938, refused to disbelieve. He was a man of faith. His Catholicism, rather than narrowing his moral vision, seems to have allowed him to embrace the possibility of human goodness, and the goodness of primal feeling. Sweetness.

Poems in another extended sequence, *Tristesses* (actually a good deal less sad than the elegies could I advise Jammes I would suggest that he switch the titles), are more like what one would expect from a Symbolist poet, more image driven, more compressed, more frankly erotic, more filled with surprise and synesthesia—that Symbolist technique that points toward the notion of the unified sensorium. Still there is that faith in the natural world and in the elemental truth of feeling, as in "Poem II:"

> She went to the bottom of the meadow,
> and because it was all in flower
> with plants whose stems thrive in water,
> I picked them, those water-sodden plants.
> Soon, wet through, she climbed to the top
> that meadow all in flower.
> She laughed and shook herself with the
> awkward grace of a young girl unused to her body.
> The look she gave was like lavender.

She was "wet through" and gave a look "like lavender." Purity again, a singularity beyond analysis, an absolutely physical sweetness, wedded to plants, water, the seasons, the meadow, the earth. Throughout the sequence declarations of sadness and longing (though not as frequent as in the elegies) are always somehow validated by a fresh and embracing imagery, and the other way around: balance.

The *Quatrains* sequence is even closer than *Tristesses* to Symbolist practice. The very brevity of the poems makes this likely, since there is less volume by which the declarative may be balanced, but we do find it here occasionally as well, as in "Vertigo:"

> The emptiness around me forms mountainous heights,
> the sheep scatter, all this makes me tremble.
> My dream: a little hamlet tucked away
> over the church at sea level, a balustrade of tranquility.

Granted, "All this makes me tremble" is more active declaration than "Suddenly I am overcome with sadness," but at least it keeps the speaker's physical and emotional presence in the poem. We also find here the connection between the natural world and the erotic, as in "Purity:"

> As countless swarm the wisteria, despite
> frost on the walls, hunting nectar, lost,
> a stray cluster confusing the air, the pale sun,
> your blond hair. Everywhere white.

Francis Jammes published widely and prominently throughout his long career, yet he has achieved something like the quality of a secret. Some of this obscurity may be attributed to his determination to live in his native Pyrenees, far from Paris and the other great centers of cultural foment. Part of it is due to the pastoral settings and content of many of his poems, which look back to an earlier age in which the orderly goodness of the natural could be believed in and form the basis for an approach to life. Still, his work is likely to outlive much that was written in praise for or protest against the passionate brutality, color, genius, and sorrow of the twentieth century and its great, essentially urban moil. His poems will go on reminding us that the natural, the erotic, the sacred, all forms of the primal, form one thing; just as faith, purity, and feeling combine, even in the face of death, loss, age, and disappointment, to form a vision of the essential sweetness of existence.

CHRISTOPHER HOWELL has published ten collections of poems, most recently *Gaze* (Milkweed Editions, 2012), and *Dreamless and Possible: Poems New & Selected* (University of Washington Press, 2010). Other recent work may be found in the pages of *Field*, *The Gettysburg Review*, *Pleiades*, and *Image*. Since 1996 he has taught at Eastern Washington University's Inland NW Center for Writers, in Spokane, where he is also director of Willow Springs Editions and director and principal editor for Lynx House Press.

Francis Jammes and Anglo-American Modernism

Benjamin Johnson

In the early twentieth century, a Francophile reader of English-language literary magazines would have been very likely to know the name Francis Jammes. Such a reader might have seen Ezra Pound announce in a series of articles he wrote about French poetry in 1913 that "I am inclined to think that Jammes is the most important poet in France,"[1] or Amy Lowell declare in *Poetry* in 1916 that Jammes "compels our love" and "has had a powerful effect on the younger generation."[2] In the years leading up to the First World War, Jammes was considered important enough to be praised repeatedly by the leading lights of the emerging Anglo-American avant-garde, and to be ridiculed by critics of modern poetry. Up through the 1920s, he remained a mainstay of anthologies and a centerpiece of scholarly surveys of contemporary French poetry.

And then, at least in the English-speaking world, he vanished. Search engine results should obviously be taken with a grain of salt when presented as scholarly evidence, but they tell a striking story

---

1. Ezra Pound, "Paris," *Poetry* 3, no. 1 (1913): 28.
2. Amy Lowell, "Miss Lowell on French Poets," *Poetry* 7, no. 4 (1916): 206.

about the course of Jammes' reputation over the last 100 years. A search of the Modernist Journals Project, a database of 24 English and American "little magazines," reveals sixty articles mentioning Jammes from 1900 to 1922. By way of comparison, a search for Jammes' contemporary Paul Valéry returns fewer than ten results. The MLA database, however, shows how drastically reputations can change. Since 2000, 76 works of English-language scholarship list Valéry as a subject heading, whereas only one scholarly article has been published in English on Jammes in the twenty-first century (and that article is about Jammes' reception in Italy). Jammes has disappeared from the story of the development of American Modernist poetry, even as many of his French contemporaries, most obviously the Symbolists, retain central roles in that same story.

It is not my goal to argue that Jammes had the same level of influence on Anglo-American poetry as Mallarmé, Rimbaud, or Valéry—quite clearly, he did not. However, at an absolutely critical moment in the formation of Modernist poetics—specifically, from roughly 1910 to 1920—Jammes was a frequent topic of discussion in the magazines where Modernism was incubated, and for poets like Pound and Lowell, Jammes proved rhetorically useful as an important contemporary French poet whose aesthetic sensibility resembled their own. These poets saw in Jammes a writer who, even if he was hardly a proto-Imagist, was nevertheless a widely respected artist whose commitment to *vers libre* and a direct, unadorned style exemplified many of the principles they sought to introduce into Anglo-American poetry. During these same years, other writers in little magazines were far more critical of Jammes. Initially, these negative responses came from avowed anti-Modernists, but toward the end of the decade, important avant-garde figures like Richard Aldington and Pound himself also began to critique Jammes for his post-conversion piety and the quality of his later work. The evolution of Jammes' reputation among Anglo-American Modernists is not only a forgotten story of cosmopolitan cultural exchange, but also an important example of the way English-language Modernism developed in the little magazine era. The cheerful simplicity that many Anglo-American Modernists had initially praised in Jammes' poetry came to be valued less and less as the aesthetics of Modernist poetry evolved away from Imagism in the years during and after the

First World War. In this essay, I describe Jammes' reception among English-speaking readers in the early part of the twentieth century—first among academic readers, and then among the Modernist avant-garde—and I also posit some guesses about why he disappeared so rapidly from the consciousness of Anglo-American readers and writers of modern poetry.

In the early decades of the twentieth century, Jammes ranked among the contemporary French poets most frequently read in English-speaking nations. In the 1927 *Anthology of Modern French Poetry* published in New York by Alfred A. Knopf, Jammes is given as many pages as Mallarmé, and more than Rimbaud or Claudel. The era's two most prominent English-language book-length studies of contemporary French poetry, Mary Duclaux's *Twentieth Century French Writers* and Amy Lowell's *Six French Poets*, both devote a section to Jammes. Interest in Jammes was also present in academia, where scholarly articles on Jammes were written by the likes of Albert Schinz of Smith College, author of several major studies of French literature, and Joseph Warren Beach of the University of Minnesota, an important professor of Modern literature who wrote one of the first scholarly monographs on Henry James.

These writers' praise of Jammes tends to center on the idea that his poetry is simple, rustic, unsophisticated, and joyful. For Schinz, Jammes' books "tell his happy enjoyment of the nature of God, of his unsophisticated sharing in the sacraments and rites of the Church."[3] Beach and his colleague Gustave van Rooesbroeck argue in a *Sewanee Review* article titled "Francis Jammes, Primitive" that Jammes "gives us candidly his impressions of his daily life, with little concern to please the public or the critics, without torturing his words to fit the forms prescribed by theorists."[4] Lowell repeatedly calls Jammes "bucolic"[5] and Duclaux is so fond of her formulation "Faun turned Friar" to describe Jammes that she uses the same

---

3. Albert Schinz, "The Renewal of French Thought on the Eve of the War," *The American Journal of Psychology* 27, no. 3 (1916): 310.
4. Joseph Warren Beach and Gustave van Roosesbroeck, "Francis Jammes, Primitive," *The Sewanee Review* 28, no. 2 (1920): 173.
5. Amy Lowell, *Six French Poets* (New York: The Macmillan Company, 1915), 232.

phrase twice.[6] Duclaux sums up the tenor of much early writing about Jammes when she writes, "His verse is still fresh with the fragrance of wild thyme newly wet with dew. He continues to sing his happy valley, with the mountain towering up behind, right into the blueness of the sky."[7]

Given the terminology deployed in the previous paragraph, it might seem odd to us that writers like Pound and Lowell considered Jammes modern. And indeed, one of the key issues running through early criticism on Jammes is the question of categorization: where, exactly, does he fit into the narratives of French poetry and of Modernist poetry? His partisans certainly understood him to be anti-Symbolist, or at least post-Symbolist. Van Roosbroeck writes in the introduction to Jammes' poems in Knopf's *Anthology* that "the very human, very simple, and yet personal note of his poems was quite antipodic in 1893-96, when they first appeared, to the then prevailing esoteric, complex, and tortured manner of the Symbolists."[8] The more divisive issue of categorization, though, was the seemingly simpler question of whether or not Jammes is "Modern." For Duclaux, Jammes is fundamentally resistant to Modernity. Commenting on Jammes' increasing piety in his later work, she writes, "He is at great pains to assure us that he is not a reformer, a philosopher, a Modernist, or a free-thinker. We should never have suspected this gifted and ingenious singer of being any kind of thinker! He is a poet, a most indubitable poet, and that is enough."[9] Elsewhere in her book she calls Jammes "seemly" and an "author for the family circle,"[10] which certainly fits the broader picture she paints of a conservative poet. Beach and van Rooesbroeck, for their part, see the question of Jammes' Modernity as more vexing. On the one hand, they note that "If one considers his technique, the deliberate freedom of his verse…one will answer at once: he must be a modern of the

---

6. Mary Duclaux, *Twentieth Century French Writers* (New York: Books for Libraries Press, 1966), 173.

7. Ibid., 110.

8. Gustave van Roosbroeck, "Francis Jammes," in *An Anthology of Modern French Poetry*, ed. Gustave van Roosbroeck (New York: Alfred A. Knopf, 1927), 31.

9. Duclaux, *Twentieth Century French Writers*, 114.

10. Ibid., vii, xvi.

moderns, an innovator, a revolté. The same answer will probably be made in view of his daring naturalism, and even of the directness of his manner, his extreme informality."[11] However, in the next paragraph, they argue that there is something "medieval" about Jammes, and that "He has renounced—in so far as he ever had it—the critical unrest of our time. Scientific facts do not disturb him."[12] Beach and van Rooesbroeck see Jammes as a formal innovator who is nevertheless unconcerned with Modernity itself, and they make a compelling case that he should therefore be grouped with other artists, ranging from Gaugin to Vachel Lindsay, in a "cult of the Primitive. And is not that the latest thing in all the arts?"[13]

It is the poets we now think of as "Modernist" who made the most vociferous case that Jammes is not only modern, but an exemplary figure of the era. Pound, especially, celebrates Jammes in these terms in a lengthy piece he wrote for the English weekly *The New Age* in 1913 as part of a serialized study of contemporary French poetry. In response to the criticism that Jammes is merely a writer of light witticisms, Pound writes:

> a man reading Jammes about A.D. 2500 might get a fair idea of our life, the life of A.D. 1913. I think he might get a fairly intimate sense of this life and be drawn into it very much as I have been drawn into some study of medieval conditions by the reading of Dante. I do not for a moment compare the four volumes of Jammes with the *Divina Commedia*. M. Jammes' work resembles the Musee du Louvre far more than it resembles the Acropolis; but after all, the highest symbols of national desire and of our present civilization are our great picture galleries. Each city must have one, from Edinburgh to Indianapolis, just as in the Middle Ages or in classic times each city would have had its cathedral or its abbey or its temple. I admit that the sensation of transcending one's time is wholly and thoroughly delightful. Nevertheless, if a poet manages to be, in sort, the acme and epitome of his time and of the civilization from which he

11. Beach and Van Roosbroeck, "Francis Jammes, Primitive," 182.
12. Ibid., 183.
13. Ibid., 185.

is sprung, I think it is all that we may justly demand of him.[14]

It might seem odd to praise a poet by pointing out how little he resembles Dante, but in his typically circuitous way, Pound praises Jammes. When he says that Jammes is the poetic equivalent of a picture gallery rather than a cathedral, Pound implies that Jammes' poetry presents the reader with a temporal series of sensory impressions rather than a timeless space for meditative depth. Pound's tone is obviously a bit playful—one rarely sees the word "Indianapolis" in a truly self-serious work of literary theory—but behind that playfulness, his choice to define Modernity in terms of a preference for perceptual immediacy over absolute perfection lets him implicitly connect Jammes to a variety of Modernist literary ideas, most notably the philosophy of T.E. Hulme and the aesthetic sensibility of Imagism.

As Pound analyzes specific Jammes poems, his terms of praise are remarkably similar to the language he had used to describe Imagism in several now-famous manifestoes he had published over the previous two years. Writing of Jammes' poem "J'allai à Lourdes", Pound says:

> You will see that the author does not sentimentalise. He portrays a situation full of feeling, or emotion, and, if you like, of sentiment. He distorts nothing. He does not try to make the thing any more pathetic than it was. He does not weep any imaginary tears, and he does not call upon the reader to weep any…You might, if you like, say that the next poem is irony. Yet is it precisely that? It is simple and adequate statement. The author does not forbid you to add to it. It is simple and adequate statement.[16]

14. Ezra Pound, "The Approach to Paris," *The New Age*, October 9, 1913, 695-6.
15. Hulme was a frequent contributor to *The New Age* in these years, so Hulmean ideas would not have been foreign to the magazine's readership. For more on Hulme's influence on Modernist aesthetics in the years before World War I, see Michael Levenson's *A Genealogy of Modernism* (Cambridge: Cambridge UP, 1984), especially pages 42-7.
16. Pound, "The Approach to Paris," 695.

The distaste for artificial sentimentality that Pound identifies in Jammes is certainly of a piece with what Pound had written in the closing paragraphs of "Prolegomena," which had appeared early in 1912 in *Poetry Review*. There, he had argued that modern English poetry needed to move away from the "sentementalistic, mannerish" poetry of the nineteenth century and toward a poetics that would be "austere, direct, and free from emotional slither."[17] Similarly, his praise of Jammes' ability to write the "simple and adequate statement" recalls his advice to poets to use "no superfluous word, no adjective which does not reveal something" in his essay "A Few Don'ts by an Imagiste," which had been published only seven months earlier in the March 1913 issue of *Poetry*.[18] At bottom, Pound praises Jammes for his "direct treatment of the thing," and in so doing he enlists Jammes—one might even say that he drafts Jammes—into the Imagist movement.

Amy Lowell, in her 1914 lecture series *Six French Poets*,[19] goes even farther than Pound in identifying Jammes as a poet whose work resembles her own sensibilities. It is not surprising that, among American Modernists, it was Lowell who most valued Jammes. Of the major Imagists, Lowell wrote most often of pastoral scenes or images, and she tends more often than the others to introduce a personal or emotional note into these poems (an "I" who thinks briefly and elliptically of a "you").[20] Lowell's desire to develop a poetics that would be modern but not necessarily urban or impersonal made Jammes a natural choice for her to put forward as a significant French influence on American poetry (just as Eliot's desire to develop an urban, complicated poetics led him to identify Baudelaire and Mallarmé as key precursors). Consider how the mixture of

17. Ezra Pound, "Prolegomena," in *Modern Literary Criicism 1900-1970*, ed. Lawrence I. Lipking and A. Walton Litz (New York: Atheneum, 1971), 23.
18. Ezra Pound, "A few Don'ts by an Imagiste," *Poetry* 1, no. 6 (March 1913): 201.
19. The lectures were published in book form in 1915.
20. This is just to say that Lowell is pastoral and personal in her imagist work more often than H.D., Williams, or Pound; not that these other poets do not have important poems that are pastoral or personal or both, or that Lowell did not write compelling urban poems.

romantic longing and self-deprecation in Lowell's "The Bungler" resembles Jammes' "Écoute, Dans Le Jardin," or the way that each poet uses nature imagery less as a symbol than a demonstration of desire in "Aubade" or "La Maison Serait Pleine De Roses." There are obvious differences here—Jammes mimics the gentle amble of speech where Lowell at her best captures the velocity of just-processed sensory impressions—but there are enough commonalities in their versification, tone, and subject manner to make it clear that Lowell is the most "Jammes-like" of the major poets of the Anglo-American avant-garde, which might explain her commitment to defining Jammes as a representative modern poet.

In the first paragraph of her chapter on Jammes in *Six French Poets*, Lowell asks "What is this modern spirit which distinguishes Francis Jammes and Paul Fort from the men of the *Symboliste* group? If I were obliged to define it in a word, I should say that it was 'exteriority' versus 'interiority.'"[21] She goes on to argue that most of the major French poets of the nineteenth century—she singles out Baudelaire, Verlaine, and Musset—were united by a conviction that "a man who did not find the world dust and ashes was a philistine,"[22] and that furthermore "they were a pack of individualists, egoists, living in a city, and inoculating one another with the microbe of discontent."[23] The Symbolist poet, she argues, "examined his mental processes under a microscope until he was like the gentleman in the story who had everything but 'housemaid's knee.'"[24] But then Lowell turns, and contends that in the twentieth century, "exteriority" has become "the characteristic modern touch. By this extremely awkward word, 'exteriority,' I mean an interest in the world apart from oneself, a contemplation of nature unencumbered by the 'pathetic fallacy.' It is the reason of the picture-making of the modern poet."[25] Here, Lowell, identifies an Imagist aesthetic with Modernity, and she further argues that "the 'modern' poet dares to be happy and say so."[26] And it is Jammes, of course, whom she believes embodies this

21. Lowell, *Six French Poets*, 213.
22. Ibid., 213.
23. Ibid., 214.
24. Ibid., 215.
25. Ibid., 215.
26. Ibid., 216.

modern aesthetic of exteriority and happiness: "Francis Jammes," she writes, "is the poet of contentment, of observation, of simplicity. He is the poet of hills, and fields, and barns, not of libraries and alcoves."[27] For Lowell, poets like Baudelaire and Verlaine were urban, bookish, and sickly (note her evocations of microbes and bursitis), but Modernity will be healthy and open to observing the world, as exemplified by Jammes, whose "poetry blows across the scented verses of the 90's like the wind from one of the snow-capped peaks of his native Pyrenees."[28]

If Lowell is correct that the case for Jammes as an important modern poet rests on the idea that modern literature will be happy, uncomplicated, pastoral, and not interested in labored self-investigation, then it becomes easier to understand why Jammes disappeared from the story of Modernism. I don't want to be too hard on Lowell here—her identification of "exteriority" as a key feature of modern literature obviously has a basis in Imagism, Cubism, Futurism, and a variety of other avant-garde movements, and most of the signal works of complex psychological interiority that we now see as central to the Modernist period had either just begun to appear serially as Lowell was giving her lectures in 1914 (e.g., *Á la recherché du temps perdu*; *A Portrait of the Artist as a Young Man*) or were still years if not decades away from being written (e.g., Yeats' *The Tower*; the major novels of Woolf and Faulkner). And who could have guessed in 1914 that Eliot, Kafka, and Beckett would come along to make the "discontent" Lowell identified in Baudelaire look like a mild cold? In the early years of the Modernist period the question of what exactly it would mean to be modern was still up for grabs, and the definition Lowell imagines—the definition that would have made Jammes a central figure—lost out to a very different conception of Modernity.

Specifically, Lowell's definition lost to a definition of modern literature that prized difficulty and density, two qualities rarely attributed to Jammes. As Leonard Diepeveen has argued in *The Difficulties of Modernism*, the contention that difficulty is an essential quality of serious modern literature begins to be widely articulated around

---

27. Ibid., 217.
28. Ibid., 217.

1915,[39] and is essentially codified in 1921 when Eliot states in "The Metaphysical Poets" that "it appears likely that poets in our civilization, as it exists at present, must be difficult. Our civilization comprehends great variety and complexity, and this variety and complexity, playing upon a refined sensibility, must produce various and complex results."[30] Given that the prevailing winds of literary taste were shifting toward poets like Donne and Herbert, it is easy to intuit how Jammes would have fallen out of fashion.

Still, the details of how he fell out of fashion are instructive. Many Anglo-American critics expressed dissatisfaction with Jammes' work even in the years of his relative ascendancy, but the content of those negative reactions evolved over the course of the 1910s. In the pre-war years, Jammes' detractors in the literary press generally attacked him for the very breaks with poetic tradition that Pound and Lowell praised, but by the end of the 1910s it was key figures of high Modernism who expressed increasing disenchantment with Jammes because his simple, straightforward style no longer read as innovative.

The lengthiest attack on Jammes in the English press in the pre-war years was a parodic piece by Beatrice Hastings that appeared in *The New Age* one week after the 1913 article by Pound discussed above. *The New Age* was known for publishing authors who openly disagreed with one another, and no one embraced this culture of disputation more than Hastings, who used a wide array of pseudonyms to debate other *New Age* contributors including, quite often, herself under yet another pseudonym.[31] As Pound published his series on French poetry throughout the Fall of 1913, Hastings (using the pseudonym "T.K.L.") followed him each week with a parody of his previous week's article. Her parody of Pound's piece on Jammes lauds the poet in a voice both wide-eyed and absolutely self-assured.

---

29. Leonard Diepeveen, *The Difficulties of Modernism* (New York: Routledge, 2003), xiii.
30. T. S. Eliot, "The Metaphysical Poets." *Selected Prose of T. S. Eliot*, ed. Frank Kermode (New York: Harcourt Brace and Company, 1975), 65.
31. The best piece on the culture of internal debate at *The New Age* with a particular focus on the Hastings-Pound dispute is Ann Ardis' "The Dialogics of Modernism(s) in *The New Age*," *Modernism/Modernity* 14, no. 3 (2007): 407-34.

"Reader," she opens, "when I began these articles I had no notion that there were so many Frenchmen!"[32] And although T.K.L. had praised many French poets over the course of her series, Jammes, she assures us, holds a special place:

> But to Jammes I allot a special niche upon the new Parnassus, for Jammes is more uniquely unique than—I had nearly said—than any other living French poet, but we must conserve our plaudits—any of the above-mentioned unique poets; he makes things more his own than I can express; he has perfected the new perfection of being a man in the street; he is your very ordinary self, your office-boy, your office, your telephone, your insurance card, and your stamp. He is the great eliminator of the abstract, the general, the universal, the essential, the transcendental—but he is the grand recorder of the Detail! Jammes has a written a novel in verse detailing life in every small town of France. Think of that![33]

Hastings mimics Pound's assertion that Jammes' value lies in renouncing the transcendent for "simple and adequate" renderings of the everyday, and her claim that "he has perfected the new perfection of being a man in the street" takes Pound's argument to absurd extremes to suggest that the interest in the mundane shared by Jammes and the Imagists leads to an art that, even if perfectly rendered, will do nothing more than reflect our own banality back to us.

Hastings spins this lampooning of Jammes' realism into a broader send-up of the avant-garde as she mock-analyzes her own parody of Pound's description of Jammes' verse-novel *Existences*:

> The poor woman sobs "Gueu, gueu, gueu…" thirty five times. Jammes writes them all down. It is all exactly like a realist novel and done to the life. Jammes is a Detailist, and every single one of Madame's noises is to him a natural and mentionable Detail. Now I think of Naturalism. Shall I

32. "T.K.L." (Beatrice Hastings). "All Except Anything," *The New Age* (October 16, 1913): 733.
33. Ibid.

therefore call Monsieur Jammes a Naturaliste? Why not? He mentions everything. He is a Mentionaliste. He is part of our normal life. He is a Normaliste. He produces in his poems the effect of conversation. He is a Conversationaliste. He says something—so few people do! He is a Somethingaliste. And now, perhaps, we have Jammes.[34]

Jokes at the expense of obscure literary movements and the French are of course the stock-in-trade of anyone who wanted (or wants) to insinuate that the Modernist emperor has no clothes, but Hastings does a marvelous job mocking the era's proliferation of manifesto-toting movements with her parade of increasingly ridiculous "isms" and "istes" (full disclosure: "Mentionaliste" makes me giggle every time I read it). None of this is fair to Jammes, who was never particularly concerned with the prevailing winds of literary fashion, but Hastings clearly associates him with the avant-garde in large part because Pound was one of his major champions. She proceeds along these lines to lampoon Jammes' use of free verse, and she implies that he is a flash in the pan as she concludes, "I don't think I shall ever say another word about him."[35]

Hastings' putdowns of Jammes and the avant-garde were certainly acidic, but far more damaging to his long-term reputation would be the fact that key Modernist writers and magazines began to cool on his work as the 1910s advanced. One can already hear rumblings of this in 1914, when poet-critic Muriel Ciolkowska, writing in the *Egoist*, calls Jammes "that charming pot-au-feu poet, unreal realist, the *bourgeois* psalmodist whom the bourgeois does not read, who chants of a world where everyone is good and kind and forgiving...He is the one poet the world has ever seen 'who is perfectly satisfied with his fate'—no doubt because he is blessed with a private income; everyone isn't."[36] Ciolkowska's attack on Jammes is a mélange of class resentments—she manages to deride him for being common, middle-class, and possessed of independent means in the

---

34. Ibid., 734.
35. Ibid.
36. Muriel Ciolkowska. "Two French Books," *The Egoist* 2, no. 1 (January 15, 1914): 37.

space of one paragraph—but she also makes it clear that Jammes' cheeriness does not fit the sensibility of the *Egoist*, which in 1914 was already on its way to becoming one of the most influential periodicals of the period.

World War I would only make Jammes' work seem less relevant to Modernist critics. In 1919, Richard Aldington argues in *Poetry* that "whether one is brutalized by the war, or tired of his repetitions, or whatever cause, [Jammes] now appears singularly lacking in charm or *éclat*."[37] Even more significantly, Jammes' very public embrace of Catholicism late in his career made him anathema to many writers, as one can certainly see when Aldington declares "in recent years he has become more and more absorbed in religion; his realism tends to the vapid, his simplicity seems artificial, his emotion has slipped imperceptibly into sentimentality."[38] When Jammes could be read as a sort of naïve realist who celebrated the pleasures of the senses in casual free verse, he looked to young, experimental writers in England and America like the poetic equivalent to Primitivism. But as the decade progressed, his religious zeal seemed out of step to a generation of writers disillusioned by war.

And ultimately even Pound cooled on Jammes. Though he continued to recommend Jammes' earliest books, and was never as vicious as Hastings or Ciolkowska, it is clear that, like Aldington, Pound was repulsed by the Catholic turn in Jammes' late career, and began to find fault with the same simplicity he had once praised. In 1918, Pound wrote a lengthy study of contemporary French Poetry for *The Little Review* that resembles in scope his 1913 series for *The New Age*. His opinion of Jammes had changed signifcantly in those five years. Pound begins his 1918 essay by praising Jammes' *Existences*, but then writes, "Only those who have read it and 'L'Angelus de l'Aube' can appreciate the full tragedy of the Jammes debacle."[39] Pound suggests that Jammes might have suffered from "some organic malady, some definite softening of the brain," or perhaps been

37. Richard Aldington, "Recent French Poetry," *Poetry* 15, no. 1 (October 1919): 47.
38. Ibid.
39. Ezra Pound, "A Study of Modern French Poets," *The Little Review* 4, no. 10 (February 1918): 41.

"broken beneath the strain of modern existence."[40] Initially, then, Pound seems to be fitting Jammes into the commonplace of the fresh young poet whose work declined in conservative adulthood, but soon Pound derides Jammes' earlier work as well. After quoting "J'aime l'ane si doux", Pound states, "the fault is the fault or danger, which Dante has labeled 'muliebria'; of its excess Jammes has since perished."[41] "Muliebria" is Dante's term for "womanish" writing in *De vulgari eloquentia*, where he contrasts it to the "tough" or "virile" language appropriate to a lofty style.[42] As Pound's essay proceeds, he accuses Jammes of "sentimentalizing," "decadence," and a "fatal proclivity to fuss."[43] Though there is also a fair amount of praise in Pound's essay, he repeatedly implies that Jammes is too soft and feminine to be taken entirely seriously by the readers of *The Little Review* circa 1919.

The reasons that Pound grew less enamored with Jammes are a microcosm of why the same thing happened with Anglo-American readers and critics more broadly: Jammes changed, the world changed, and Modernism changed. Jammes changed in the sense that his late-in-life piety and overt religiosity led to negative reviews in many influential English-language magazines that no doubt colored perceptions for years to come. The world changed in that the bucolic pleasures of Jammes' poetry were out of step with the social and political upheavals of the early twentieth century. And finally, and perhaps most significantly, English-language Modernist poetry changed because Imagism, which could easily define Jammes as an important precursor, gave way to more complicated forms of experimentation and epic ambition that made Jammes seem less and less like a proto-Modernist. Perhaps if Lowell had been canonized as the central poet of Modernism, Jammes would be more known to Anglo-American readers today. But instead it was Eliot, more than anyone else, who set the terms of what it meant for a poet to be modern and innovative, and due to his influence, a group of French

---

40. Ibid.
41. Ibid., 42.
42. Glauco Cambon, *Dante's Craft: Studies in Language and Style* (Minneapolis: University of Minnesota Press, 1969), 199.
43. Pound, "A Study," 42-4.

poets very different from Jammes would come to be seen as precursors to the Anglo-American avant-garde. That said, Jammes has a place in the story of English-language poetry. Certainly he was a vital influence on Lowell, but more importantly, he presents a telling example of how Modernism did not arrive in the world fully formed, but rather evolved out of a series of arguments about who and what was worth reading.

BENJAMIN JOHNSON is an Associate Professor of English at the University of Central Missouri. He earned a PhD in English at Rutgers University. His scholarship on Modernist poetry has appeared in *The Wallace Stevens Journal* and *Arizona Quarterly*, and he has an article on Marianne Moore forthcoming in *Texas Studies in Literature and Language*.

On the Contemporary Significance of Jammes' Landscapes

John Gallaher

Francis Jammes, though an important poet both in his own right and as an influence on other poets, didn't fit in well with the narrative of the age of either early twentieth-century French or American poetry as it came to be written. At the onset of Modernism though, his stock was looking good, as Ezra Pound, in the early years of the century, wrote in a letter to Harriet Monroe, "I think if our American bards would study…Francis Jammes for humanity, and the faculty of rendering one's own time…there might be some hope for American poetry."[1]

Even as late as1957, Jammes was firmly enough in the American literary consciousness, that Kenneth Rexroth could write,

> Amy Lowell, Sandburg, H.D., Pound, Marianne Moore, William Carlos Williams, Wallace Stevens—all the major poets of the first quarter of the century owed far more to

---

1. Quoted in Malcolm Bradbury, "The American Risorgimento" *Modernism: 1971-1984*, ed. Tim Middleton (New York: Routledge, 2003), 110-32.

Apollinaire or Francis Jammes than they did to the whole body of the English tradition. In fact, the new poetry was essentially an anti-English, pro-French movement—a provincial but clear echo of the French revolt against the symbolists.[2]

Such a view of the American Modernist period is not so much ignored these days as it is taken for granted in a general way, and specific names of poets and examples of direct influence have faded into a kind of fuzzy background aura, the "French influence."

In the rare instances when French poets do get named as influences on twentieth-century American poets, though, Jammes usually fails to make the list, where once he would have headed it. So what happened to cause Jammes, between 1957 and now to fall out of the conversation, even as poets such as Wallace Stevens, greatly influenced by Jammes and other French poets of Jammes' generation, have risen in stature? And, a more interesting question to me, what might be found in Jammes' poetry now—as mode, lesson, strategy—that might give us a new way to approach composition? These questions are tied together, and can be illustrated by looking closely at a few of his poems alongside Stevens', which enlightens both poets as well as some of the affiliation between Stevens and John Ashbery.

First, Wallace Stevens' "Anecdote of the Jar":

I placed a jar in Tennessee,
And round it was, upon a hill.
It made the slovenly wilderness
Surround that hill.

The wilderness rose up to it,
And sprawled around, no longer wild.
The jar was round upon the ground
And tall and of a port in air.

2. Kenneth Rexroth. *World Outside the Window: The Selected Essays of Kenneth Rexroth*. ed. Bradford Morrow (New York: New Directions, 1987), 51.

It took dominion every where.
The jar was gray and bare.
It did not give of bird or bush,
Like nothing else in Tennessee.

And then a similar landscape with focal point in the opening stanzas of Jammes' "Fourth Elegy":

When you asked me to compose an elegy
for this abandoned country where the high wind
makes the sad white birch trees rustle in the grey sky,
once again, in the green shade of the wet thickets,
I saw a rumpled dress with long ribbons.

From the green grass of the park, under the cold dead sun of October,
a broken Diana rose up like a fountain.
The false pistachio trees, the red hazel nuts,
the lacquer-trees, the laurels and the roses
produce a sad and beautiful passageway at the horizon
where blue emanations stain the sky.

At once, Stevens' debt to Jammes is apparent. The human object (jar / dress) dominates and comes to order the landscape, and the landscape is imbued with the emotions of the solitary viewer. For Stevens, the jar reveals the "slovenly wilderness" that rises up to it, "no longer wild." The made thing, the jar, tames and characterizes the landscape as does the made thing, the "rumpled dress" of Jammes. For Jammes this focal point imbues the landscape with a reason for being there, to be the "sad and beautiful passageway" for this "broken Diana." Everywhere in Jammes' work can be found such instances, where a Diana (or a Susanna, as Stevens might say) could be said to "sing beyond the genius of the sea" in Stevens' iteration, and how this importing of the classical female into the landscape for both poets puts them at odds with the thinking of the time. For Stevens, this move is countered by his insistence on the ordering abilities of the imagination, which fits him more comfortably into the version of Modernism we've come to know. Jammes, however, takes this movement back to the person and personality of his solitary watcher. Take the women in the garden in Jammes' "Elegy Two," for instance, and the way this thinking is mirrored in numerous poems from Stevens:

Cherished memories sweeter than lemon balm
fill my joyous heart, which remains sad,
like a garden full of young girls.

This "obscure music" as Jammes calls it later in the poem, though also a fundamental approach of Stevens', shows the great and final difference between the poets. The fecundities of Stevens are pushed into the logos of imagination while for Jammes these fecundities reside in the pathos of memory (for instance, at no time in Stevens do we find a line like "fill my joyous heart"). Both poets see the human organizing the landscape, though for Stevens, as he states in the *Adagia*: "Life is an affair of people not places. But for me it is an affair of places and that is the trouble." This same organized landscape, for Jammes, however, is always turning back to the social, to the self and a circle of friends and acquaintances, either as elegy, memory, or as a way to define the self. One could imagine Jammes saying the inverse of what Stevens says above, that perhaps life is an affair of places not people, but for him it is an affair of people and that is the trouble.

This philosophical distancing of Stevens is why his poetry has been described as "Wittgenstein in verse." Jammes' desires were more personal, and that's made all the difference for his reception. As the twentieth century wore on, the use of the emotional and personal landscape in the ways that Jammes uses them fell out of favor, feeling more and more rural in a world turning more and more to cities. By the time American poets "discovered" the power of the personal in the late 1950s, Jammes, though a major contributor to its development, went unnoticed, as he was (if thought of at all) relegated as a footnote to the French Surrealists or American Modernists.

Stevens did know of Jammes' poetry, and together they illustrate the sort of thinking that was in the air at the time, and both can give us examples of how perception can proceed from an encounter with the landscape. Nor is "Fourth Elegy" the only example of an affiliation between Jammes' and Stevens' manner of thinking. "No ideas but in things" both poets enact in their work, but also with similar echoes through the personal, the vagaries of perception, of "no things but in ideas," and how the self—the moods of the self regarding the landscape—enacts the landscape, imbuing it with its moods which are the moods of the self. Consider the cry of Steven's peacock in "Domination of Black":

Out of the window,
I saw how the planets gathered
Like the leaves themselves
Turning in the wind.
I saw how the night came,
Came striding like the color of the heavy hemlocks
I felt afraid.
And I remembered the cry of the peacocks.

And this, the self imprinted on the landscape, from Jammes' "Third Elegy," which has affinity with both the Stevens poem and with the sort of self revelation one finds in a poem such as Robert Lowell's "Skunk Hour":

Dearest, if you have the answer, come and tell me.
Tell me why, when I am in the depths of despair,
why does it seem like the trees are as ill as I am?
Will their death come with mine?
Will the sky die? Will you?

It's an interesting mix of tones and relationships one finds in the poetry of Jammes, where at one point it seems almost Wordsworthian (a poem such as "Fifth Elegy" comes to mind, where "It's sweet October, the time of the lit pipe. / A robin sings to the pale muddy sun") only to steer through a close analogue of Stevens only to then abruptly stop the action and shift its tone, as in "Elegy Two" with the late aside: "And besides that, what else do I do today?" that would be perfectly at home in the poetry of any of the poets associated with The New York School. "A mythology reflects its region," Wallace Stevens writes in the late poem of the same name, and unintentionally makes a case for the difference between his poetry and the type of poetry Jammes wrote:

> In Connecticut, we never lived in a time
> When mythology was possible—But if we had—
> That raises the question of the image's truth.
> The image must be of the nature of its creator.
> It is the nature of its creator increased,
> Heightened. It is he, anew, in a freshed youth
> And it is he in the substance of his region,
> Wood of his forest and stone out of his fields
> Or from under his mountain.

So what can be found in the poetry of Jammes? We are currently living in a time when mythology is possible, and now that we are, there is the renewed possibility that the sorts of images Jammes created can be newly embraced for their elemental power. The peopled landscape—it's a social-rural reminder that we are all also of this earth and what is and will be found in us is also to be found in the landscape.

JOHN GALLAHER is the author of four books of poetry, most recently *Map of the Folded World* (University of Akron Press, 2009), and, with the poet G. C. Waldrep *Your Father on the Train of Ghosts* (BOA Editions, 2011). His next book will be the book-length essay-poem *In a Landscape*, coming out in 2014 from BOA. He also co-edits for *The Laurel Review* and GreenTower Press.

An Invisible Hand: On Francis Jammes

Jaswinder Bolina

Francis Jammes was a country bumpkin momma's boy living and writing nearly a thousand kilometers removed from the whizbang literary scene of the Parisian Modern.[1] Alternately, Francis Jammes, widely admired in Paris literary circles, was a Pyrenees mountain man living happily apart in the Basque borderlands between nations and centuries.[2] This double-vision version of Jammes might help explain why his poems move so freely from expressions of mournful longing to those of a clear-eyed, bucolic tranquility, why they exhibit a grunge-rock-worthy angst for the past in the elegies and a bodhisattva's contentment with the present in the quatrains. This is poetry that evokes more than one sympathy, which is what writing at its best ought to do. In this, Jammes' poems attempt what a lot of poems attempt: a totalizing of the human condition. Of course they do, but they do it without being reductive.

While his work centers on romantic love and existential doubt, features ample natural and pastoral imagery, and traffics in the

---

[1]Or so say French critics and biographers like Robert Mallet.

[2]This according to scholars like Jean-Pierre Inda.

bleeding-heart lyricism of the Romantic poets that precede him, Jammes tends to shy away from declarations of the Truth-is-Beauty variety. Instead, strong assertions—in the elegies especially—are often undercut by implicit questioning. The apparition of certainty in his poems is counterbalanced by a complicated ambivalence, sorrows counteracted by unexpected playfulness, and the move towards melodrama dissuaded by a disarming directness of voice and frankness of tone. All this to say that in Jammes' work, the tall ship of nineteenth-century poetry seems to be arriving at the shores of twentieth-century irony. Here's the final stanza of the "First Elegy":

> I think about you. The day is fading like that day
> I saw you in my old country parlor.
> I think about you. I think about the mountains of our birthplace.
> I think about that Versailles where you took me walking,
> while we recited verses, sad and moving in step.
> I think about your lover and I think about your mother.
> I think about those rams which, on the edge of the blue lake,
> waiting for death, bleated as their bells rang out.
> I think about you. I think about the pure void of the heavens.
> I think about endless water, the clarity of fire.
> I think about the dew that glistens on the vines.
> I think about you. I think about me. I think about God.

The writing here is astonishingly poignant, and while the listing in these lines does seek to totalize the elegy's subject—French Symbolist poet Albert Samain to whom the poem is dedicated—Jammes never tries to explain the nature of loss or ameliorate his experience of it. He simply inhabits Samain's absence while that absence makes the speaker's memory of his friend all the more concrete. That memory culminates in this last stanza's free-verse cascade of imagery, which ends finally in an open interrogation of subject, self, and God.

The significant point is that Jammes doesn't reach for resolution here. He arrives instead at a final ambivalence. In The "First Elegy," the concluding litany begins in a rustically banal parlor; moves through every manner of Samain's relations as friend, son, and lover; through the grandeur of Versailles and recitations of poetry; through a landscape perpetually tinged by the inevitability of death. It rises even to the allegorical bombast of heaven and the elemental, which is where an elder Romantic poem might find its conclusion; but Jammes continues onward to the hapless-beautiful image of dew on the vines and his entirely inconclusive thoughts about the human condition. The irony in this final downshift is unlike that of the Romantics; I'm thinking of the sardonic last lines of poems like Shelley's "Ozymandias" or Keats' "This living hand…" Instead, Jammes engages in a more contemporary brand of the literary ironic by evoking the grammar of resolution—the subject thinking about BIG ideas like *you*, *me*, and *God*—without being able to offer any hint of a resolution. Where, in the Romantic, thought can shape reality, in the modern and for Jammes, thinking itself becomes the subject.

More interesting than all of that, though, is the way the poem directly addresses its subject. This might be what best distinguishes Jammes' work from that of his contemporaries. There are poets who write to the ether and those who write to the other. Jammes is of the second persuasion. In the intimacy of its address, his "First Elegy"—among many of the poems collected in this volume—feels quietly spoken to someone real, someone close. It "addresses itself to one person (other than the poet himself), thus evoking overtones of love without destroying love's life-giving vulgarity, and sustaining the poet's feelings towards the poem while preventing love from distracting him into feeling about the person,"[3] which is to say that Jammes seems to anticipate Frank O'Hara's rightly celebrated "Personism" manifesto by half a century prior to O'Hara writing it. This probably isn't an accident. O'Hara deeply studied the very schools of French Symbolist and Surrealist poetry that Jammes is credited with bridging in his work. If the former became famous for the easy familiarity of his voice and his poems' mock-conversational tone, it's possible he found an ounce of inspiration in the work of the latter.

Here's Jammes' "Fourteenth Elegy" that reads like an early rendition of O'Hara's "Poem (Lana Turner has collapsed!)":

Darling, you said. And I replied, Darling.
It's snowing, you said. It's snowing, I said.

---

3. Frank O'Hara. "Personism: A Manifesto." *Selected Poems*, ed. Mark Ford (New York: Knopf, 2009), 247.

Again, you said. And I replied, again.
Like that, you said. And I said, like that.

Later you said: I love you. And I, I love you more.
Lovely summer is over, you said to me. It's fall,

I said. And our words had got out of synch.
At last one day you said: Oh dearest, how I love you…

(It was a day when the long fall was fast losing its grip.)
And I said back to you: Say it again…and again…

I don't mean to suggest that I've uncovered the hitherto unrecognized pilot light of O'Hara's genius. O'Hara's oeuvre is too varied and voluminous, his innovations too original to assign to the influence of any one figure, but Jammes must be there somewhere in the DNA, and this poem suggests as much. This is significant because of the tremendous sway O'Hara's work has had over a great many of us writing today. Discovering Jammes, then, is something akin to hearing Woody Guthrie for the first time after years of listening to *Bringing It All Back Home* or like that day you discover Grandmaster Flash or Gertrude Stein or the Marx Brothers and have a sudden sense of where everybody else got some part of the bright idea.

Reading Jammes' poems now, they feel uncannily familiar, as if they'd always been there, an invisible influence pervading contemporary poetry like gravity bending a limb. This is probably because he was read so widely a century ago by those poets who forcefully defined much of the Modern—both Stéphane Mallarmé and Ezra Pound adored his poems—and no doubt known, too, to the Francophile poets of midcentury American postModernity. Somehow, though, his significance has been obscured by time, his work mostly lost to those of us a continent and a century removed from his moment. For me, reading this selection of his poems, then, is to experience the glee of discovering a missing link, a bridge between New York in the 1950s and Keats' and Shelley's Rome of the early 1800s.

Jammes is, however, more than a dead relic in the fossil record. As should be expected of any master, he has lessons for those of us writing today. His work is formally rangy. He experiments with poems long and short, with prolonged sequences and terse vignettes. He dabbled, too, in playwriting, or at least in playwriting as poetry, and wrote a number of successful, as yet un-translated novels. He accomplished all of this by resisting allegiance to any one particular aesthetic, form, or genre. His success in doing so suggests that it might be better for writers to avoid the kind of factionalism and rivalries that have come to define the American literary scene of the last half century. Further, throughout his work, there's a force of personality with so much to say. There's earnestness and urgency. In reading his work, I feel compelled to write lines as effusive and palpable as,

> The house would be full of roses and wasps.
> In the afternoon, we would hear the bell ringing for vespers;
> and grapes the color of translucent stones would appear
> to be sleeping in the sun, below the crawling shade.
> How I would love you there!"

In reading Jammes, I feel compelled to write with such keen immediacy. In reading Jammes, I feel compelled to write.

JASWINDER BOLINA is the author of *Phantom Camera* (New Issues, 2012), winner of the Green Rose Prize, and *Carrier Wave* (Center for Literary Publishing, 2007), winner of the Colorado Prize. He teaches in the MFA program at the University of Miami.

In Praise of Fauns

Kathryn Nuernberger

Francis Jammes achieved the height of his fame and accolades between 1896 and the early years of the twentieth century when he was a young bachelor living in Belle-Epoque Paris, travelling abroad in Algeria on occasion with Andre Gide, fully embracing the pantheistic philosophy underlying the Symbolist movement, and seeking transcendence in the arms of real and imagined women, in defiance of the Catholic mores of the Pays Basque region of rural France where he was born and raised. In his translation of Jammes' 1901 play, *The Naked Girl*, Barry Gifford echoes the approbation the young Jammes received in his own time from the likes of Gide and Alain-Fournier, writing in the introduction, "His reality was his imagination, it was there he lived and made love with flowers, bees, trees, perfect virgins."[1]

But, as the story of Jammes' reputation goes, he could not remain true to his identity as a countercultural faun of the Parisian gardens. The voice of an oppressive mother, ringing in his ears and out of his superego, compelled him in his thirties to seek spiritual

1. Francis Jammes. *The Naked Girl: A Poem/Play*, trans. Barry Gifford and Bettina Dickie. (Berkeley: The Workingman's Press, 1977), 2.

guidance from the devoutly Catholic and politically conservative Paul Claudel, return to the provincial Pays Basque, marry a dull woman for whom he had no great passion, and embrace with piety and propriety the Catholic faith of his community. Robert Mallet, a prominent mid-century critic and biographer who helped secure Jammes' place in the French canon, wrote of the dissolution of Jammes' first great love affair, a failed engagement that, it has been suggested, precipitated his return to the bourgeoisie. Mallet writes,

> Francis Jammes had experienced for the first time a sense of the fullness of love during an affair he would have liked to turn into marriage. But he encountered the most categorical refusal on the part of his mother, who felt that this union was unreasonable and incompatible with certain conventions of bourgeois respectability.[2]

The narrative that Jammes chose propriety over poetry is widely accepted among those who are familiar with Jammes' work and it is the major explanation for Jammes' position at the margin of the literary canon in the postmodern period. However, this is a flawed narrative that overlooks how much of his highly regarded early work reflects a deep attachment to the Pays Basque and how entangled his later descriptions of transcendental feelings are in post-industrial political convictions. His return to Catholicism and the writings that emerge from the experience are similarly a bi-product not only of religious feelings, but of his commitment to and expression of solidarity with a marginalized homeland.

The French Critic, Jean-Pierre Inda, attempted to complicate the simplistic accounting of Jammes' mature work, and to demonstrate that the religious overtones in this work were not dogmatic tracts, but rather were nuanced and political works of literature. In

---

2. "En effet, un an auparavant, Francis Jammes avait éprouvé pour le première fois un sentiment de plénitude amoureuse au cours d'une liaison très romanesque qu'il aurait voulu transformer en mariage. Mais il s'était heurté au plus catégorique des refus de la part de sa mère qui jugeait cette union déraisonnable et incompatible avec certaines conventions de respectabilité bourgeoise." Robert Mallet, *Francis Jammes* (France: Editions Pierre Seghers, 1964), 38.

Francis Jammes et le pays Basque, he reframes the narrative, writing,

> Jammes has his themes. Themes that filled his first works:
> a nature without pomposity but teeming with a slightly
> acidic sap, a love that also tortures the dreamer, the calm of
> provincial villages—these are themes carried forward into
> his rediscovered faith, along with sympathy for a human
> brotherhood on a common journey, pity for those who suf-
> fer, piety towards the saints and the Host.[3]

Inda insists in *Francis Jammes: du Faune au Patriarche* that his writings
after his return to his Basque homeland are thematically nuanced
works of literary philosophy. One must "[c]onsider the evolution of
his fifty years of poetry, an evolution directed not only by his return
to the faith, but by the enrichment of all of his human experiences."
Inda goes on to call for "a portrait of the texts that is more clear,
more thoughtful, and more complex."[4]

You can see Jammes' trademark approach to nature and longing
in his early play, *The Naked Girl,* which chronicles a young man's jour-
ney through the verdant forest in search of he knows not what.
Goaded on periodically by the encouraging nudges of the character
"Little Old Woman," he finds himself in the final scene gazing upon
a young woman bathing. "You are the naked soul and flesh. You are
the truth whose limpid perfume has blossomed on my lips. What is
this pure dream I am going to live?" While Belle Epoque readers

---

3. "F. Jammes a ses thèmes. Thèmes qui emplissent les premières œuvres
: une nature sans emphase mais pleine de sève un peu acide, un amour
aussi torturant que rêveur, le calme provincial de petits villages…. thèmes
qu'apporte la foi retrouvée : sympathie pour les frères humains, piété
pour les frères souffrants, piété envers les Saints, et l'Hostie." Jean-Pierre
Inda, *Francis Jammes et le pays Basque.* (Lyon : Presses Academiques, 1952),
72.
4. "De l'évolution qui se dessine en ces cinquante ans de poésie – évolu-
tion commandé non seulement par le retour à la foi du poète, mais par
l'enrichissement de toute une expérience humaine – nous aurions aimé
donner une image plus nette en un texte plus composé et plus dense."
Ibid., x.

and the several generations of critics in the mid-twentieth century that followed, doing the work of compiling the new canon into anthologies, seem to have had few objections to the use of a naked girl as a symbol of man's transcendent connection to the beyond, such figurative language grates against third-wave feminist ears. If only the young poet in this play had been content to possess not an objectified body but the mystery of the forest he wandered through, as the little old woman directed his eye,

> Look: the tiniest grasses appear one by one. There's the golden euphorbia, the blue speedwell, the moss. Feel them living in their sweet and simple goodness. They cannot be heard. The dew is their voice. Their souls will gently fade away in a few days. They're the modest ones. They perform an unknown duty, as do we.

As Jammes matured, this well-wrought, but troublingly possessive male gaze increasingly gave way to the voice of a transparent eyeball in the Emersonian tradition, observing without judgment and content to linger in mystery as the character of the little old woman does.[5] This style flourishes in the *Four Books of Quatrains*, published between 1922 and 1925.[6] Together the books illustrate an evolution in the direction of an ecofeminist style that illustrates a relationship to the land woven with socially progressive political engagement. Instead of the all-too-familiar story of a young man who grew old and sold out, Jammes' return to the Basque Country provides the example of a young revolutionary who revises and refines his art and politics as he matures. The protest against hegemony that was so erotically figured in his youth becomes full-bodied (intellectual, emotional, and spiritual) in his later work.

---

5. "Standing on the bare ground,—my head bathed by the blithe air, and uplifted into infinite spaces,—all mean egotism vanishes. I become a transparent eye-ball; I am nothing; I see all; the currents of the Universal Being circulate through me; I am part or particle of God." Ralph Waldo Emerson, *Nature*. (San Francisco: Chandler Publishing Company, 1968), 13.
6. All translations from *Four Books of Quatrains* are by Kathryn Nuernberger.

In the quatrains, his women are refreshingly less symbolic than those in his early work and embody nuanced human attributes, while men enter the poems not as reflections of the poet who writes them, but as characters in their own right—friends, neighbors, community leaders, and others whose lives intersect with and shape the speaker's own. This transformation is starkly apparent in "To My Goddaughter Sylvette Guillon-Verne," who a younger Francis Jammes might have described as a generically naked muse fallen into a poet's erotic embrace.

To My Goddaughter Sylvette Guillon-Verne

You returned from the depths
of the earth, the sky, then the dew
evaporated off lilies, not even damp,
not even, close as it was, smudged with dirt.

The girl has fallen from the sky, the images of lilies and the depths of the earth suggest a brush with death, but the poem does not lament her tarnished innocence (whether it be sexual innocence or the innocence of one's mortality). Instead Jammes chronicles her journey as if it were an adventure through the earth, the sky, and the dew of the flowers, an adventure another Verne might have led her on. And he celebrates her return to the family, careful to note that if she has lain with Hades, it has not sullied her. The pagan liberties of exploration and self-discovery he granted himself in his youth are now proffered in this poem to his goddaughter.

Or in another quatrain for a daughter, we see Jammes celebrating not femininity in the abstract, but the scrappy personality and carefree attitude of a unique individual.

Portrait of Françoise Jammes

Pudgy as a rose-bud,
my youngest in the garden,
socks slipping down, chats away
with the dog, the doll, and bench.

Here we see Jammes subvert the old clichés about girls and rose-buds by describing his child and the iconic feminine flower as "pudgy." He emphasizes her socks slipping and her imaginary games in an attempt evoke a child so busy being her carefree self that she has no time or need to embody someone else's longing.

Jammes' project in the *Four Books of Quatrains* is to document the lives of people in the Basque Country, and that project requires him to see women as characters with inner lives instead of as symbols for an idea a poet has. Here's a portrait of a mother grieving her child:

Croup

Today it's death, yesterday was living.
Since we last saw you in the school, holding
a toy one gives to children—Oh mother,
your boy is gone, the toy remains.

In fact, there's no "idea" in this poem, only the fragmented stutter of speaker observing this grief with a deep empathy that no carefully complete sentence could adequately express. In another quatrain, Jammes sensitively inhabits a limited third-person perspective, documenting how insecure women from the fields might feel coming into town, a place where they are most acutely aware of the elegant muses someone of their gender might be expected to embody.

Farm Wives in the City

From the rain and the mud they descend,
from hills of gorse and broom sheared by bovine
teeth, jamming their troublesome strong fingers
in white gloves, they have all the allure of a plow.

It would be easy to interpret "the allure of a plow" as an insult, but in the quatrains surrounding this one, Jammes praises the work of the plow and the people who do this labor. He makes his readers long for such "troublesome strong fingers." In this poem Jammes seems to be anticipating Francoise d'Eaubonne's argument in *Le Féminisme ou la mort* (1974) for an ecofeminist understanding of the connection between exploitation and domination of women with that of the environment. With a humanist attitude towards the second sex that was ahead of his time, Jammes turns from the erotic pantheism of his youthful poems towards a subtext of political solidarity with the Pays Basque and resistance against the industrial age's centralizing impulses. Though not expressly concerned with the egalitarian treatment or depictions of women, his interest in social justice for a rural agrarian community seems to have honed his attention to the lives of people marginalized by the economic engines of globalization, including those of women.

Citizens of the Pays Basque felt the pressures of the industrial age on their folk life and economy acutely in the early years of the twentieth century. Once the Kingdom of Navarre, the Pays Basque was split in the sixteenth century into French and Spanish territories. However, for centuries the region maintained a unique cultural identity and at times militantly independent spirit that was renewed in the nineteenth century by the European Romantics who embraced nationalist aesthetics. Throughout the early part of the twentieth century the Spanish portion of the Pays Basque struggled under increasingly oppressive regimes—Jammes' death in 1938 coincided with Franco's rise to power. This tension between Basque culture and Spanish governance would later give rise to a Basque Independence Movement. Readers can see Jammes' attention to and concern over the increasingly unstable politics in a number of poems. In "Les Infantes," Jammes plays with the Spanish double entendre—infantes are child heirs to the Spanish throne, but also the names of the foothills to the Pyrenees that divide the Spanish side of Basque Country from the French side.

Their Royal Highnesses, The Infantes

With a song of grief echoing from out of his court
the southern wind comes whipping around the violet coats,
shadows pleat them, a little mountain range
flowing from the Pays Basque into Spain.

On the French side of the border the political climate remained stable, though the technologies of industrialization stressed the traditional economies of the Pays Basque, and the Parisian center of French culture turned an increasingly blind eye to the art and culture of the provinces. There are more than a few quatrains about threshing and the simple feasts that surround this communal labor. "Minotaur" is a poem haunted by the imposing presence of the latest automated farm equipment that might spell the end of such rituals.

Minotaur

They spent all yesterday working on the thresher
and couldn't get it to hum.
But look at her now, how she swells and bellows
devouring sheaves of hair, plaited and luminous.

In the early twentieth-century Basque regions, the culture was comprised of folk arts almost entirely interwoven with the rituals, feasts, stories, and music of the Catholic faith. This was in marked contradiction to the anti-clerical sentiment in other parts of the country that led to the 1905 French law on the separation of the church and state, which crippled the Catholic religion as an institutional force in public life and granted ownership of all religious buildings to the State. While the separation of church and state has become a widely accepted principle in contemporary France, its initial implementation during Jammes' lifetime was perceived as a traumatically destabilizing event in those communities whose social structure was organized around the Church.

In a time when an already insular community felt threatened by external secular forces, Jammes' decision to return to the faith of his childhood allowed him renewed access to Basque communities that was not available to outsiders. By fully embracing the cultural life of the Pays Basque, Jammes was able to write about his homeland not with the preciousness of a member of the removed urban elite, but as one who is part of the landscape and the work of people whose livelihood is directly tied to that land. Consider, for example, "Far from the Salons," which describes the unique landscape of the region with more grit than romance, while playing with the Christian icons of lambs and shepherds, complicating any easy understanding of the theology of sacrifice.

Far from the Salons

It was a brutal day in the chaparral
when we saw the wild horses passing
and that dog tied up, reluctantly picking
at a dead lamb the shepherds abandoned.

This poem contemplates the problem of suffering in God's creation based on a direct encounter with blood and death that could only be theorized about at the table of a Parisian salon. While those salons were proving so inspiring to many of the twentieth century's most significant luminaries, Jammes was attending feasts and masses with peasants who had no publishing connections to share. But, as "The Banquet" illustrates, Jammes' artistic interest in the preservation of a Basque cultural identity, required he sit instead at these tables, draped in the colors and symbols of the Basque flag.

The Banquet

The ceremonies at this table feel almost holy,
what with a blood-red table cloth adorned in lilies,
the flag beaten by the winds,
an old Basque song drowning out the clinking dishes.

Many Catholic doctrines of social justice are built around the Beatitudes, which bless the poor and the meek, so Jammes' attention to marginalized characters can easily be misinterpreted as mere catechistic recitations. However, his depictions of poor, meek, hungry, and persecuted figures, always emphasize the uniquely Basque attributes of their lives and their struggles. As a professed Catholic, Jammes would have believed these were the children of God, but the quatrains employ the scriptural allusions to function aesthetically as an appreciative gesture for the Basque folk arts.

The Pays Basque Francis Jammes knew was a unique cultural ecosystem. More than a few of today's writers are familiar with similar sub-cultures, working as they do in the various provinces of Academia. Of course contemporary writers have to be willing to give up those provinces as soon as the degree is completed or the fellowship concludes, the contract expires or the funding is revoked. But Jammes wouldn't move on to the next gig. It may be that in the twenty-first century such longing to commit to a particular landscape is a fantasy laced with tediously romantic nostalgia. It may be that any sense of regional identity in the postmodern age is a pitiful gasp before the cosmopolitan tide of agribusiness, monocropping, and multinational conglomerates. It may be that localvore homesteaders with backyard chickens are delusional fauns much like the young Francis was imagined to be. Be that as it may, Francis Jammes' oeuvre should not be dismissed as catechistic or compromised, because these are poems to help contemporary readers get through whatever the next wave of Industrialism brings.

KATHRYN NUERNBERGER, a poet and co-editor of this volume, teaches Creative Writing at the University of Central Missouri where she also edits poetry for *Pleiades: A Journal of New Writing*. A former high school French teacher, she holds a PhD in Creative Writing from Ohio University and an MFA in Poetry from Eastern Washington University. Her collection of poems is *Rag & Bone* (Elixir, 2011). She lives on a small farm in rural Missouri.

About the Series:

Volumes in the Unsung Masters Series are published once a year and feature work by, and essays on, unjustly neglected or out-of-print writers. Each volume in the series is distributed free to *Pleiades* subscribers with the summer (June) issue. Unsung Masters Series books are also available through Small Press Distribution.

Volume 1, *Dunstan Thompson: On the Life & Work of a Lost American Master*, edited by D. A. Powell & Kevin Prufer, 2010

Volume 2, *Tamura Ryuichi: On the Life & Work of a 20th Century Master*, edited by Takako Lento & Wayne Miller, 2011

Volume 3, *Nancy Hale: On the Life & Work of a Lost American Master*, edited by Dan Chaon, Norah H. Lind, & Phong Nguyen, 2012

Volume 4, *Russell Atkins: On the Life & Work of an American Master*, edited by Kevin Prufer & Michael Dumanis, 2013

Volume 5, *Francis Jammes: On the Life & Work of a Modern Master*, edited by Kathryn Nuernberger & Bruce Whiteman, 2014

Forthcoming volumes:

Volume 6, *Catherine Davis: On the Life & Work of a Lost American Master*, edited by Martha Collins, Kevin Prufer, & Martin Rock, 2015

Volume 7, *Beatrice Hastings: On the Life & Work of a Modern Master*, edited by Benjamin Johnson, 2016